P9-DSX-310

Circles of Exclusion

Circles of Exclusion

The Politics of Health Care in Israel

Dani Filc, MD

With a Foreword by Quentin Young, MD

ILR Press

an imprint of

Cornell University Press

Ithaca and London

Copyright © 2009 by Cornell University

All rights reserved. Except for brief quotations in a review, this book, or
parts thereof, must not be reproduced in any form without permission in
writing from the publisher. For information, address Cornell University
Press, Sage House, 512 East State Street, Ithaca, New York 14850.

First published 2009 by Cornell University Press

Printed in the United States of America

Library of Congress Cataloging-in-Publication Data

Filc, Dani.
    Circles of exclusion : the politics of health care in Israel / Dani Filc ;
with a foreword by Quentin Young.
        p. cm. — (The culture and politics of health care work)
    Includes bibliographical references and index.
    ISBN 978-0-8014-4795-2 (cloth : alk. paper)
    1. Medical care—Political aspects—Israel.   2. Medical policy—
Israel.   3. Minorities—Health and hygiene—Israel.   4. Aliens—
Health and hygiene—Israel.   5. Social medicine—Israel.   6. Medical
economics—Israel.   I. Title.   II. Series: Culture and politics of health
care work.

    RA395.175F55   2009
    362.1095694—dc22   2008047452

Cornell University Press strives to use environmentally responsible
suppliers and materials to the fullest extent possible in the publishing of
its books. Such materials include vegetable-based, low-VOC inks and
acid-free papers that are recycled, totally chlorine-free, or partly composed
of nonwood fibers. For further information, visit our website at
www.cornellpress.cornell.edu.

Cloth printing   10   9   8   7   6   5   4   3   2   1

To my late father, David, and my mother, Sara, for their example of personal integrity, intellectual curiosity, and love

CONTENTS

FOREWORD

As I sat down to read Dani Filc's *Circles of Exclusion,* I expected to learn a great deal about the Israeli health care system. What I did not expect was to find that this tiny country enmeshed in a seemingly intractable conflict in the Middle East would have so many lessons for the world's most powerful nation—the United States. Several pages into this courageous book, it became clear that the issues Dr. Filc describes hold great relevance for those grappling with America's ongoing health care crisis. The crisis in Israel and that in the United States are the result of the impact of neo-liberal market policies that are currently being imposed on health care throughout the globe. In both countries we see a decline in concern and funding for public health and the exclusion of the poor racial and ethnic minorities from increasingly privatized health care systems in which the survival of profit-making enterprises seems to be the paramount concern.

Using the Israeli example as a case study, Dr. Filc raises questions about the very future of egalitarian notions of health and social services in affluent industrialized societies that have become more concerned with the wealth than the health of the species. And he does so by tackling a subject that is of interest to anyone—Jew or non-Jew—who is concerned with the fate of the first and only Jewish state in the world.

Circles of Exclusion tackles these issues with both passion and scholarly rigor. Dani Filc is a practicing physician, and an Israeli citizen who has a firm identification with the Israeli state. He is also a scholar and a social justice/public health activist and advocate. Dr. Filc in fact emigrated to Israel from Argentina and was promptly integrated as a citizen and a professional under the Right of Return policy, which awards citizenship to any Jew who desires it. He knows what it means to have voluntarily chosen the land of Israel as his own. As someone who tried to serve the poor and underserved in his own native country, he was also deeply impressed with the commitment to egalitarianism and social solidarity he encountered when he first came to Israel several decades ago.

Today he is deeply concerned about how the current market-oriented health care theories are undermining the very ethical concerns and principles that were embedded in this early Zionist model. In spite of its collective roots, the Israeli health system now increasingly mimics some of the worst aspects of the American privatized system.

Dr. Filc grounds his analysis on classical public health theory. For the poor and elderly Jewish citizen, for the Bedouin in the unrecognized villages, for migrant workers, and for Palestinians in the occupied territories, myriad resources—financial allocations from the state, high-tech and tertiary facilities, safe water and sewage control, specialty services, roads and transport to medical facilities, as well as the social determinants of health such as education and decent employment—are all difficult or impossible to access.

For a public health advocate like myself, the message of this book is crystal clear. Obsessive preoccupation with free-market formulas are intensifying social and health care problems in industrialized countries, not resolving them. Of course, Filc shows us how this has happened in Israel, which because of its history puts a very specific spin on the problems of the poor, the old, racial and ethnic minorities, and the new migrant working class that crisscrosses the globe. Nonetheless, in Israel and elsewhere, preoccupations with profit are crowding out concerns for the classic social determinants of health and, as Dr. Filc points out over and over again, are not saving money but actually wasting it.

The final echoes contained in this book regard the inevitable lessons about the links between military occupation, health care, global health, and global peace. Indeed, as Dr. Filc explores the close connection between the Arab-Israeli conflict and American military support, anyone who has been fighting for a more just and accessible health care system in the United States cannot help taking note. Not only does Dr. Filc elaborate how health care has become another weapon in a seemingly endless conflict, he also points out the tragic consequences of spending billions on military hardware and personnel rather than on the provision of social services that could become tools for peace rather than war making. The emergence of military checkpoints and creation of border walls that have made services available only in Israel inaccessible to patients in the Occupied territories, have also created another group denied access to health care—migrant workers recruited from global populations desperate for employment.

This book greatly adds to our knowledge of the consequences of neoliberal policies in health care. It is also a critical contribution to the scholarship on the development of the Israeli state. Although it contains a strong critique it also contains a message of great promise.

For Dr. Filc the early Zionist solidarity represented an assertion that health care is a human right as well as a deep commitment to the tenets of burgeoning knowledge about public health. He helps us understand the wisdom that public health and prevention yields far greater gains than an exclusive focus on either therapeutic or market-based medicine. Finally, he promotes the concept of health care as a human right and helps us understand that by expanding on this human right, health care itself can be a tool for peacemaking in a region whose future holds either peril or promise for the entire globe.

QUENTIN D. YOUNG, MD, MACP

Clinical Professor of Preventive Medicine and Community Health at the University of Illinois, Chicago, and Past President of the American Public Health Association and National Coordinator of the Physicians for a National Health Program

ACKNOWLEDGMENTS

In writing this book I am indebted to many people. My colleagues and friends at Physicians for Human Rights-Israel have been, and still are, an inspiration. In their ceaseless struggle against violations to the right to health they have formed a community to which I am proud to belong.

I am grateful to those teachers and colleagues at the university who have taught me to ask questions and seek answers. Whereas the list is a long one, I owe professors Uri Ram and Adi Ofir a special debt.

While the faults and errors you may find in this book are my own and entire responsibility, the book's completion owes much to the support, intelligence, patience, and enthusiasm of Suzanne Gordon, coeditor of the series. Anything I can say will not express how grateful I am for her help.

Finally, the most special debt I owe is to my family—my children, Gal, Ioni, Or, and Nir, who endured the period of the writing with love and humor; and my wife, friend, and companion, Myri, for all that I have learned from her and for many years of mutual love.

Circles of Exclusion

INTRODUCTION

Four Stories of Exclusion

My patient was as perplexed as she was outraged. "You can't do it? What do you mean, you can't do it?" she asked angrily. "I've been going there for years and years for my heart checkup! And now you're telling me I have to start all over again at a new office, with a new doctor? No way!" she exclaimed as she stormed out of my office.

Ms. Levana Malka,[1] a sixty-year-old retired assistant kindergarten teacher who lived in Givat Hatmarim—one of the poorer sections of Tel Aviv—had cardiac valve disease since she was a child and developed hypertension in her fifties. To monitor and manage her condition she needed periodic checkups. From the time she developed her illness, she was insured at Kupat Holim Clalit—the sick fund run by the General Workers' Union.[2] When she was a teenager, she became a regular patient at a cardiology outpatient office at a public hospital and had continued to visit the same office, year after year, decade after decade, ever since, and she felt safe there. As the medical director of her neighborhood's primary care clinic, I knew that she preferred to continue receiving care and follow-up in a place where she was well known. But even though I understood her anger and felt as frustrated as she was, I couldn't do anything to help her.

Due to both changes in public hospitals' billing systems and financial pressures, Kupat Holim Clalit no longer allowed us to refer our patients to certain public hospitals for their follow-up. This meant that patients like Malka had to find a different cardiologist at a different institution. For Malka—whose life as a patient was centered at a particular institution, with its familiar staff, treatment, and follow-up—learning that she would be forced to change doctors, nurses, and her hospital was a shock that made it even harder for her to cope with her chronic illness.

The situation was especially frustrating for her because her condition and age prevented her from switching to a financially more stable sick fund with better access to specialists' care. Moreover, like most residents of the Givat Hatmarim neighborhood, Malka could not afford private care.

Givat Hatmarim is located in what used to be the city of Jaffa and has become part of the Tel Aviv–Jaffa municipality. Predominantly Arab, Jaffa is one of the few areas in Israel where—albeit with some segregation—Arabs and Jews live together. But it is also one of the poorest parts of the unified city. Except for those living on the sea—in a section that is being gentrified—most of its residents struggle to make ends meet. Public services are not well developed and public investment is scarce, which leads to severe social problems. Givat Hatmarim (the Hill of Dates) is predominantly Jewish, but its residents are not much better off than Jaffa's Arab population. Since the mid-1980s, cuts in public spending have intensified the preexisting problems of this largely low-income population and created a crisis in the public health care system.

* * *

I signed the petition without too much hope. Physicians for Human Rights–Israel, a human rights organization composed mostly of health care workers, was demanding that the state ministries connect the houses of two sick old men—Mr. Ahmad al Atrash and Mr. Shauki al Sana—to a source of electricity. Sixty-nine-year-old Ahmad and seventy-eight-year-old Shauki are Israeli Bedouins who reside in the unrecognized villages in the Negev desert, and both suffer from chronic obstructive pulmonary disease (COPD). Some 84,000 Bedouins live in forty-five villages unrecognized by the Israeli state as a result of a conflict about ownership of their land. Bedouins have lived on their land for centuries, yet the Israeli state does not recognize the Bedouins' ownership claims of significant areas of the Negev desert and has tried to pressure residents in these forty-five villages to move to seven Bedouin cities and renounce their claims to any ownership rights to the lands on which their villages were built. To pressure the Bedouin population to move, the state does not provide the villages with basic infrastructure, such as electricity, water, and sewage.

For Ahmad and Shauki this means that they will not receive the treatment their lives depend on. To manage their COPD, they must use bilevel positive airway pressure (BiPAP) treatment. Twenty-four hours a day, a machine provides artificial positive pressure that keeps the pulmonary alveoli open and thus helps to overcome the intrinsic positive pressure that hinders breathing. Their doctors have stated that they need BiPAP therapy to survive. Obviously, BiPAP cannot function without electricity, but the inhabitants of the unrecognized villages are not connected to electricity, and neither Ahmad nor Shauki can afford a generator. If the two men lived in one of the villages the Israeli government has recognized, getting this treatment would be no problem. As citizens of Israel, both Ahmad and Shauki are covered by National Health Insurance and are entitled to BiPAP. Lack of electricity, however, represents an insurmountable obstacle in their care. Physicians for Human Rights petitioned the Israeli government to connect both patients' houses to electricity. Our petition was refused, and their clinical situation deteriorated.

*   *   *

Alejandro's mother smiled wearily. She looked at me, trying to find some faint glimmer of hope. Alejandro, a slightly plump ten-year-old, was born in Israel to Colombian parents. He spoke both Spanish and Hebrew fluently and had become his mother's Hebrew translator. Despite the fact that he was born in Israel, due to the structure of citizenship in Israel he could not become an Israeli citizen and thus enjoy full access to all the benefits of the Israeli health care system. For Alejandro this was a devastating problem. He suffered from Legg-Calve-Perthes' disease—a disease that affects the femur bone in children. It begins with a limp, as the bone suffers a process of necrosis, and it can cause an irreversible deformation of the femur's head, which would result in a permanent limp. His condition required surgery. However, in the late 1990s, the National Health Insurance law did not cover children of migrant workers, even if they were born in Israel. Unlike many migrant workers, his mother managed to purchase private health insurance, but the plan did not cover chronic conditions such as Alejandro's. For noncitizens, the costs of hospitalization in the Israeli public health care system were prohibitive, especially for migrant workers employed in low-wage service work.

Alejandro came to Physicians for Human Rights' Open Clinic for migrant workers for regular checkups, while we tried to find a public hospital that would agree to operate on him for a low fee. In the meantime, Alejandro's limp, as well as his prognosis, was getting worse. Finally we reached an agreement with the Ichilov hospital: They would operate for a significantly reduced fee. The agreed-on costs still represented a real burden for Alejandro's mother.

*   *   *

Before entering Kalkilya, in the West Bank, part of the Occupied Palestinian Territories (OPT), our taxi passed by Azoun, a village a few kilometers south of Kalkilya. The crossroad connecting the road to Azoun with the main road leading to Nablus was closed by a fence with a heavy padlock, blocking Palestinian cars coming from Azoun from access to the main road. Ambulances taking patients to the hospital in Nablus had to travel across unpaved roads. To reach the hospital, a patient needed not just one ambulance but two—one to carry the patient from his or her house to the blockade, and a second, which waited at the other side of the blockade, to take the patient to the hospital, some twenty miles away. As we were watching, the drivers lifted the patient out of the first ambulance and carted the patient over the blockade, from one ambulance to the other. Unmanned fences and blockades exist not only at Azoun but all along the West Bank, limiting patients' access to health care services as well as the access of health care personnel to their patients. Ambulances are delayed at the checkpoints; people in need of treatment are denied the permits required to travel from their village to city hospitals. Doctors cannot reach the hospitals they work in, nor can they get to their patients in the villages. Obstacles in access to health care add to the already poor living conditions.

As a result, the health status of the Palestinians in the OPT is much worse than that of the Israelis.

*   *   *

The four stories described above exemplify the ways in which citizenship, occupation, and the use of neoliberal, American models shape the delivery of health care in Israel and the Occupied Territories. They illustrate the health care boundaries that encircle both Israeli Jewish citizens and non-Jewish citizens living inside Israel as well as those that surround Palestinians living in the Occupied Territories. This book is a journey inside those circles of exclusion that now determine how health care is delivered in Israel and influence whether citizens, residents, and workers in Israel and the Occupied Territories are healthy or sick. The innermost circle surrounds older and poorer Israeli Jews impacted by the neoliberal transformation of their health care system. In the second circle are the Arabs. Migrant laborers who are essential to Israeli's growing global economy are in the penultimate circle, and in the outermost circle are Palestinians in the Occupied Territories.

Readers who are not Israelis may wonder what makes the exclusionary nature of the Israeli health care system unique. The health care systems of most industrialized countries exclude as well as include. Some—such as the U.S. health care system—have become world renowned for how many of their citizens do not have health insurance. Migrant workers—particularly undocumented ones—have difficulty gaining access to health care services all over the world. Similarly, Native Canadians, Americans, and Australians—like Bedouins in Israel—suffer from histories of oppression whose legacies are etched into the policies and practices of contemporary health care systems. And, of course, war and conflict wreak havoc all over the world.

So why should a reader care about this tiny country, Israel, and read about the trials of its health care system?

This question has several answers. The problems that Israel now encounters do not reflect only local health care trends and dilemmas but global ones. As we witness the outrage and frustration of Malka as she fights for continuity of care in an increasingly neoliberal, pay-as-you-go Americanized health care system, we have before us a critical example of

the power of the neoliberal model that is now seducing medical and political establishments in industrialized countries across the globe. The fact
that Israel has been seduced by this model is particularly interesting.

Although many industrialized countries such as France, the United
Kingdom, and Sweden established universal, single-payer health care systems after World War II, the Israeli health care system is one of the world's
earliest and most impressive social experiments in group solidarity. As we
will see in chapter 1, its roots were planted in the late nineteenth century,
when Zionists first came to Palestine. These settlers created a social system
in which residents—and then, after the establishment of the state of Israel,
citizens—could not conceive of putting their individual health care needs
above the needs of a collective defined religiously, ethnically, and ideologi-
cally. Their commitment created a health care system that rivaled any in
the industrialized world. Despite these collective roots, the Israeli health
care system now increasingly mimics some of the worst aspects of the U.S.
privatized health care system.

In 1950, as we shall see in chapter 1, the American preoccupation with
choice was so foreign to the Israeli imagination that a sick person wouldn't
consider visiting a physician or hospital that was not an integral part of
his or her political or social community. By the 1990s, many Israeli thirty-
somethings were abandoning their sick parents to "inferior" sick funds
(the Israeli version of the health maintenance organization) while ensuring
that they got a better standard of service in "superior" ones. The gradual
evolution of the Israeli health care system from the community to the market holds lessons for any country dealing with neoliberal challenges to social programs.

The Israeli case is important for a second reason. Work migration is a
global phenomenon, and the arrival of migrant workers in significant numbers is common in rich, industrialized countries. This influx of migrant
workers inevitably raises the question of how—and even whether—they
are going to access health care services. The answer to this question differs
from country to country. The Israeli case is of special interest because of
its restrictive definitions of citizenship and thus social entitlement—which
largely depend on ethnic characteristics.

The confluence of global processes with local, communitarian conceptions of inclusion and entitlement produces—as the story of Alejandro
exemplifies—complex forms of access to, or exclusion from, health care.

Thus, from the Israeli case we can learn more about the specific ways in which global processes interact with local institutions, practices, and beliefs, thereby enhancing our understanding of the interplay between the global and the local.

Israeli treatment of migrant workers is also interesting given the collective history of migration of the Jewish people. It is a sad irony that a country founded as a response to the suffering of constant migration, exclusion, and expulsion partially reproduces, in its health care system and wider society, an exclusionary approach to today's global migrants.

The Israeli practices that structure citizenship also shape the limited ways in which the Bedouins in the unrecognized villages access health care. Even though Israelis would claim that their ancestors were "the first nation" in the ancient land of Israel, the contemporary example of Bedouin exclusion is yet another case of how settler societies deal with first nations. The discussion of who is, in fact, the "first nation" is at the core of how the country treats non-Jewish Israeli citizens.

Finally, questions about health care in Israel inevitably touch on Israel's position at the center of one of the globe's most controversial conflicts. Although this conflict has been depicted as a "clash of civilizations," it is really a clash of some of the most critical contemporary issues—questions about democracy, fundamentalism, nationalism, and colonialism. The prolonged Occupation of the Palestine territories is unique. Its global significance is well known. What is less well known is the major role that issues associated with health care and the health care system play in the dynamic of the conflict. As we saw in the examples above and will learn more about in chapter 5, health care has been structured as an instrument that reinforces the ongoing Occupation. Moreover, the Israeli case helps us to understand the ways in which violent national conflicts interact with and reinforce the neoliberalization of society and the exclusionary characteristics of the citizenship structure. If, for example, the United States maintains an extensive presence in Iraq, the Israeli case, which illuminates how abuse of Palestinians' right to health fuels regional conflict, will contain necessary lessons about the global ramifications of local conflicts.

The Israeli case, which illustrates the many ways in which social structure and politics limit access to health care and prevent various groups from fulfilling their potential to enjoy good health, also provides a lesson about the importance of the right to health. The *right to health* has been defined in several ways. Some of those definitions are very limited. For example, some would define the right to health as having equal rights to the integrity of the body. Others would define the right to health, as neoliberalism does, only as the right to choose a health care provider (provided that you can pay for his or her services). The definition that inspires my approach is an egalitarian, universal understanding of the right to health. This conception is based on a recognition of our common vulnerability as human beings. It asserts our equal worth as human beings and assumes a basic fact: that good health is a precondition for the fulfillment of our capacities and rights. Poor health severely impairs the possibility of enjoying or taking advantage of such rights as freedom of movement or the right to political participation.

An egalitarian and universalist definition of the right to health states that every person has a claim to the amount of services and goods—including health care—needed to provide a level of health equal to another person's health, when inter-individual differences in health are the product of social organization or can be reduced by treatment; and every person has a claim to equal health care for equal needs in those cases in which individual differences in health result from natural, biological variations for which there is no treatment.

In this book I use a "right to health" perspective to analyze the different circles of exclusion in Israel and the OPT. I do so because this perspective allows us to move beyond the particular case of Israel and to critically examine not only health care systems but, more generally, social structures and social organization in different countries. The analysis of the different ways in which exclusion from health services and limitations to the right to health are structured in Israel provides us with important insights about the ways in which major global trends function both alone and in combination. These trends include the adoption of neoliberal recipes that erode the welfare state, the privatization of health care, the erosion of solidarity; ethnocentrism and nationalism; the securitization and militarization of society, prolonged military conflicts, and prolonged occupation. Each process by itself and in combination structures differential access to health care and limits people's right to fulfill their potential to enjoy good health.

In examining the Israeli case, this book is critical of the ways in which the prolonged Occupation, aspects of the Israeli institutional structure, and the adoption (and idealization) of a neoliberal, U.S.–like socioeconomic model negatively affect access to health care. Although it is a critique of certain aspects of Israeli society, my book does not, in any way, intend to question Israel's legitimacy. Quite the contrary, I write as someone profoundly identified with Israel and its society. I have chosen to live in Israel and am a deeply committed member of Israeli society. But I am convinced that, in the spirit of the Jewish people through all its history, identification and belonging cannot and should not silence the critic and undermine the longing for *tikkun*—which means to heal, to repair, to make better. Criticizing from within is a form of belonging, an expression of deep identification. Using a medical analogy, people generally raise a critical health issue—say heavy drinking or smoking—with a loved one or a friend only if they care deeply about that person. Suggesting that someone stop smoking or change his or her drinking habits is a risky business that highlights one's sense of obligation and conviction that one must speak out to help modify behaviors that are jeopardizing that person's well-being.

Although this book is an analysis of the history and contemporary realities of these circles of exclusion, it is also a personal account of my own journey and struggle—as a physician, social activist, and policy analyst—to overcome the results of these exclusionary policies. Although I am a Jew and enjoy the full benefits of Israeli citizenship, I write this book as someone who has witnessed the full weight of what poverty, prejudice, and political oppression can do. I was born in Argentina and came of age during the military Junta's dictatorship in the 1970s. I studied medicine in the Buenos Aires public university, and as a medical student I made my clerkships at different public hospitals. There I could appreciate the dedication of the medical personnel but also the severe limitations of a health care system composed of an unhealthy mix of both private and impoverished public services. I came to Israel as a member of a Zionist-Socialist youth movement group. During my first years I was a member of Zikkim, a kibbutz south of Ashkelon, where we hoped to be part of an egalitarian commune. As a kibbutz member, I worked as a physician in Ashkelon's Barzilai hospital. A few years later I moved to Tel Aviv, and in 1990, when I finished my military service, I began to work at the Kupat Holim Clalit's clinic at Givat Hatmarim. Two years later, in 1992, I became its medical director. As medical director, I witnessed firsthand how the bonds of communal solidarity were slowly eroded so that people began to experience an "Americanization" of their society and their health care system.[3] For someone born in Argentina and familiar with the characteristics and consequences of a health care system built on the differential access to health care based on social class, this was particularly disturbing. Although I was born in Argentina and became Israeli by choice, the Occupation, and the ways in which structured social injustices penetrated the health care system, made me feel torn between my deep sense of belonging to Israeli society and the shame I felt (and feel) because of this kind of inequality. This book is a product of my effort to cope with these feelings, addressing the different levels of exclusion in the Israeli health care system through study, analysis, and political activism.

Because of my own experience, I know that decent health care is embedded in and determined by political and social realities and choices. As a physician, it's not enough to have loyalty to individual patients and to abide by a code of professional ethics that is limited to dealing with such individual cases. I have seen quite clearly that an individual ethical perspective should be complemented by a broader, political conception of health as a basic human right. Because of this, I joined Physicians for Human Rights (PHR)–Israel, a nongovernmental organization (NGO) working for a universal and egalitarian implementation of the right to health. PHR–Israel began as an organization denouncing the violations to the right to health in the Occupied Territories and broadened its scope of activity to address all violations to the right to health in Israel. Yet, I was convinced that political activism, however important, should also be complemented by understanding of the social processes and structures that underlie the unequal access to health care that some of us, at least, are grappling with in Israel. This book is an attempt to identify and analyze the structural changes whose effects I was experiencing as a physician and the way they are combined with the exclusionary citizenship regime and Israel's policy in the Occupied Territories. In writing this book, I have been undoubtedly influenced by my years of activism in PHR–Israel. The universal, egalitarian approach that characterizes the organization's activities has helped shape my own approach, and in that sense I am indebted to all those people (volunteers and staff members) with whom I have shared, and still share, years of common struggle.

In addressing this task I combine my eighteen years' experience as a primary care physician and as an activist with the theoretical knowledge I acquired at a master's program in political theory and in writing a doctoral thesis on the Israeli health care system. My goal was to put my everyday personal experience as a physician into a broader political and social context. As I explored health care in Israel, I wanted to understand the different levels of exclusion and their interrelation. I wanted to look at health care through a lens that also captures the social determinants of health—nutrition, water, and housing—and that views health care as an important, but not the only, element of the right to health. Poor health does not depend only on lack of access to health care, but results from complex causes including relative poverty, work insecurity, poor education, poor nutrition, unclean water, and poor housing conditions. Exclusion, segregation, discrimination, and the resultant inability to get a good education, find a good job, and live in a safe neighborhood, create or exacerbate health problems. Health problems caused by a lack of resources are aggravated by limited access to health care services.

To look at health care in Israel more broadly, I focus on the following questions.

- What were the historical roots and original promise of the health care system in Israel?
- What caused the profound changes of the Israeli health care system—changes that are, paradoxically, both logical extensions of and departures from these roots?
- What were the main features of the process?
- How had the financing, ownership, and management of the Israeli health care system changed?
- How had such changes affected the doctor-patient relationship?
- What was the relationship among the neoliberalization of the Israeli health care system; its growing dependence on the United States; the structure of citizenship and the Occupation?

These questions structure this exploration of the Israeli health care system. As the book will make clear, some of the circles of exclusion in this system are unique to the Israeli context; others are not but have an Israeli twist. The obstacles in access to health care that have resulted from the adoption of a more market-oriented, neoliberal version of health care as well as the exclusion of migrant workers, especially undocumented ones, are common features in rich Western countries. Israel's case is especially interesting because access to health care is also structured by the way Israeli society was born and how the ideologies and social expectations of the original settlers have determined the contours of the health care system. We see this particularly when we examine how health care has been affected by the prolonged Occupation and the conflict between Israelis and Palestinians; and the geopolitical role Israel plays, especially as this has been influenced by the intricate web of relationships with the United States in which Israeli society is enmeshed. As this book reveals, one of the less known and less considered aspects of this conflict is how it impacts the health care not only of Palestinians but also of foreign workers employed in Israel and Israelis themselves.

In this book the structure of the Israeli health care system is viewed as an element within a version of Zionism that came to dominance before Israel became a state and has continued to provide the framework for the consolidation of the Israeli society and state. This view of Zionism produced a society with a strong sense of internal solidarity and a republican philosophy that drew a stark set of exclusionary boundaries (Peled 1992; Peled and Shafir 2005). The combination of the prolonged conflict between Israelis and Palestinians and the ways in which a particular view of Zionism—known as constructivist Zionism—implemented the idea of a Jewish state, defined concentric circles of belonging and exclusion that shaped the structure of the health care system and the different degrees of access to health care. As we shall see, and as Ms. Malka's case reflects, when it came to health care and other social services, this sector of social activity was determined by need and freed from the discipline of the market. Although this was a great benefit to Israeli Jews, it also created a fragmented system where status, ethnicity, and political affiliation defined different levels of inclusion and access.

Since the mid-1980s, Israel has become an integral part of the process of neoliberal globalization. As a consequence, Israeli society changed profoundly. It became wealthier (with a gross domestic product [GDP] per capita that corresponds to the developed world), but inequality increased as economic growth benefited only a small sector of the population, and the sense of republican solidarity that characterized the country eroded. The weakening of the Israeli sense of intra-Jewish solidarity, something that made Israel one of the most unequal countries in the developed world, did not dramatically alter the exclusion of non-Jewish groups. In the mid-1990s certain policy changes—such as the broadening of entitlement to children allowances[4] and the passage of the National Health Insurance law—did diminish outright discrimination against some groups—without significantly modifying the boundaries of exclusion.

As Israel became a wealthier nation and began to adopt neoliberalism, its demand for cheap labor increased. The traditional source of cheap labor—Palestinians—however, seemed far less attractive in the post–Oslo/Intifada era.[5] As a consequence, tens of thousands of migrant workers arrived in the country. At its peak, in the early 2000s, their number reached some 250,000 people (for a total population of six and a half million). Like Alejandro, they were excluded not only from the political community but also from access to most social services.

This book thus analyzes how Israel's adoption of a neoliberal model of society has combined with the existing definitions of citizenship and the prolonged Occupation to deepen the unequal character of the Israeli health care system. This analysis allows us to disentangle a number of critical issues. By exploring Israel's participation in the process of neoliberal globalization we better understand why it has developed a multitiered health care system that increasingly excludes the older and poorer like Ms. Malka. To fully understand the nature of that fractured system, it is also critical to understand how it has been affected by the evolution of the Israeli-Palestinian conflict and Israel's geopolitical alignment with the United States. The cost of the conflict limits the resources available for social investment. The development of the security industry and the political and cultural dependence on the United States have influenced the emergence of a high-tech health care industry and a high-tech driven and expensive health care system. Dependence on the United States and the political and military support of the United States have also allowed the prolonged Occupation and shaped the neoliberalization of Israeli society.

This book analyzes the interrelationship between the main characteristics of the Israeli society and the development of a multitiered health care system where class, ethnicity, nationality, and the Occupation differentially structure access to health care. Chapter 1 presents a historical overview of the development of the Israeli health care system from the prestate days to its current organization. This chapter introduces the reader to the complexities of a highly fragmented, multitiered health care system and to the various institutions and agents—the Ministry of Health, hospitals, sick funds, voluntary sector, and private sector, among others—that constitute it. It also places that system in the context of contemporary Israeli society, its socioeconomic structure, the characteristics of Israel as a political community, and the overarching role of the Israeli-Palestinian conflict and the forty years' old Occupation. As I will try to show, these are not parallel processes but interconnected ones, and their interconnection is central in the shaping of the Israeli health care system.

The second chapter analyzes the ways in which the neoliberalization/ Americanization of the Israeli health care system grounds class-based exclusion to access to health care. The chapter analyzes the various aspects of this process: the privatization of financing; the privatization of ownership of health care services; and the emergence of a new organizational culture, one imported from the business sector, within the public health care system. The chapter shows how business culture modifies the health care sector's internal organization, language, and labor relations, transforming even the most traditional core of health care—the doctor-patient relationship.

Chapter 3 describes the obstacles the Bedouins in the unrecognized villages face in accessing health care. The chapter provides one of the most radical examples of how the Israeli state has used ethnic and national characteristics to define identity and inclusion and to distribute resources that influence health status and access to health care services. We move further into the territory of exclusion in Chapter 4, which examines the plight of migrant workers who come to Israel to seek a better life and decent jobs only to find that they are shut out when they or their children need health care. With no path to citizenship, migrant workers who build the nation and contribute to its wealth are penalized if they become sick. Not only does this jeopardize their health, it creates a potentially serious public health problem.

If migrants are shut out of the health care system in Israel, the condition of Palestinians in the Occupied Territories is even worse. Chapter 5 describes the evolution of the Palestinians' health care plight under the Israeli Occupation. After addressing the history of the underdevelopment of health care services in the OPT, we see how the Israeli army utilizes access to health care services as a threat and a punishment. We learn how blockades, curfews, and checkpoints function as a planned arbitrary system that makes uncertainty a constant while severely limiting access to health care. Finally, it becomes clear that violence in the OPT is the ultimate barrier to health care.

Unequal access to health care services is not an Israeli but rather a global phenomenon. Throughout the world, inequality is not limited to the enormous gap between the wealthier and the poorer countries but exists within each society. Racism, ethnic and cultural discrimination, widening socioeconomic gaps, and the transformation of health care services into a commodity are some of its main causes. The specific ways in which these processes occur in each country are molded by that country's particular characteristics. A comparative analysis would be one way to examine these processes. The in-depth study of one society is another. Examining how the neoliberalization of health care services has occurred at the local level and interrelates with state institutions and social practices contributes to the understanding of similar processes in other countries. Tolstoy's phrase—paint your village and you will paint the world—is particularly valid in our brave new global village not only because of the similarities certain processes display in different countries but also because we cannot understand what is happening locally without understanding what is happening globally and vice versa.

This book, which studies the different levels of unequal access to health care in Israel, is about more than development of the health care system in a single country—albeit a country that plays a central role in one of the major global conflicts of our era. This book hopes to expand our understanding of the different ways in which ethnicity, nationality, or class result in exclusion from access to health care. As such, I hope to contribute to our understanding of how health care systems can set up obstacles to the very services they are supposed to provide and to encourage a strong personal and professional commitment to a universal and equal right to health.

1

The Israeli Health Care System

An Overview

A group of old men meet everyday in the waiting room of one of the Israeli sick funds. Day after day, they gossip, talk politics, argue, and joke. One day they all realize that they haven't seen Moshe, one of the regulars.

Astonished and worried, Yaakov asks Pesah, "What happened to Moshe? Why didn't he come today?"

"Well," Pesah, replies without the slightest irony, "Today he is not feeling well. He's really sick."

As with many jokes, this one reveals much about the institutions it seems to mock—in this case, the sick funds in Israeli society, especially during the country's first four decades. In Israel, sick funds were designed not only to deliver health care services but also to serve as a cornerstone in the construction of the Israeli's sense of belonging to a new society. The strong links among the sick funds (especially the Kupat Holim Clalit and the Kupat Holim Leumit sick funds), political parties, and workers' organizations gave them a central role in the configuration of individual and collective identities and in the distribution of political power and resources in the newly developing state. These political and cultural affiliations have also been part of the definition of who belongs and who is excluded in Israeli society.

Today, Israelis receive their health care from a public, single-payer system. Four public, nonprofit health organizations—called "sick funds"—are responsible for the provision of health care services. In what was from its inception a fragmented system, whose diverse institutions have little vertical or horizontal integration, actual health care services are provided by several institutions: the sick funds themselves, state hospitals, city hospitals, and hospitals belonging to nongovernmental organizations (NGOs). The current configuration of the Israeli health care system has been reshaped by the contradictory combination of a privatization process that started in the late 1970s and the legislation of the National Health Insurance law in 1994.[1]

The fact that the Israeli health care system is both public—that is, inclusive—as well as exclusive and fragmented is a result of the way it developed during the Ottoman period, the Mandate period, and the period after Israel became a state in 1948 in which health care, like all other social and political institutions—was dominated by the Histadrut (General Workers' Union). The fundamental influence on the Israeli health care system has been—not surprisingly—the conflictive process through which the state of Israel emerged. Thus, critical to any understanding of how the system works today is a consideration of Israel's history—particularly its Zionist roots.

Zionism was a reaction to centuries of prejudice and persecution that Jews faced in the Diaspora. In the late nineteenth century, Theodore Herzl, a Hungarian Jew, believed he had found a solution to the persecution of the Jews in Europe and elsewhere. Since even the most enlightened European countries exhibited periodic outbreaks of anti-Semitism, Jews, Herzl argued, should accept the inevitable. As the revisionist historian Avi Shlaim has written, "Assimilation and emancipation could not work because Jews were a nation. Their problem was not economic or social or religious but national. It followed rationally from these premises that the only solution for the Jews was to leave the Diaspora and acquire a territory over which they would exercise sovereignty and establish a state of their own" (Shlaim 2001, 2).

Herzl's Zionist vision was a product of the emergence of nationalism in Europe. For romantic nationalists, a people—whether Italian, German, Hungarian, Russian, or, in this case, Jewish—constituted an organic unity, bonded by blood and cultural links. What the Jews, like other nation's clamoring for their own state, lacked was a homeland in which they could build separate Jewish political, economic, and cultural institutions that allowed them to freely express this connection. What they needed in short was a Jewish state. Herzl himself was not committed to creating that homeland in Palestine. Uganda and even Argentina were briefly considered. But the pull of the biblical land of Israel proved too strong for many to resist, and Palestine—a place that was, Zionists insisted, "a land without a people for a people without a land"—became the location of choice. This formulation, of course, ignored the existence of the Palestinian Arabs who lived on the land for hundreds of years.

While a small number of Jews—motivated largely by religious belief—immigrated to Palestine in the eighteenth and nineteenth centuries before the Zionist movement began, Zionism spurred a more significant immigration to Palestine beginning in the 1880s. These first Zionist immigrants were largely from Eastern European countries. Most of them were secular Jews and not religious. A main current among them, inspired by different strands within the socialist tradition, dreamt of combining national reconstruction with social justice in the Jewish homeland.

Even though Palestine was far from being a Jewish state in the early twentieth century, a series of statelike institutions were set up to become, Zionist leaders hoped, the seeds of full-fledged state institutions. Some of these institutions—such as the Jewish Agency, the institution in charge of steering Zionist political action; the United Jewish Appeal, in charge of fund raising; and the Jewish National Fund, in charge of buying lands for Jewish settlement—were active mainly in Europe and the United States. Others were institutions that emerged within the Jewish community, such as the Vaad Haleumi (National Council), which was the "government" of the Yishuv, the Jewish community in Palestine; the educational network; and the *Histadrut,* the Jewish workers' organization. Provision of health care was a main preoccupation for the Jewish settlers, and health care organizations were central among the institutional framework they built.

The Ottoman Period

During the Ottoman period, until the mid-nineteenth century, "health care" was practically nonexistent in what was then called Palestine. The only hint of what one would today consider a systematic attempt to deliver health care services occurred during potential epidemics when ships and their crews were quarantined at ports and municipal medical officers supervised isolation and disinfection procedures to control potential epidemics (Reiss 1988).

With the arrival of religious missions to the Holy Land in the nineteenth century, the penetration of Western-styled health care slowly began. The first European licensed physicians came to Palestine in 1838, when the Anglican mission opened a clinic in Jerusalem. These hospitals were ready to provide care to all the residents in the region, Muslim and Christian Palestinians and Jews. However, because it feared the missionaries' intentions, the religious leadership of the small Jewish community living in Palestine (the "old" Yishuv) banned the mission's clinic. In order to meet the health care needs of the old Yishuv, the British Jewish philanthropist Moses Montefiore sent the first Jewish physicians and pharmacy to Jerusalem in 1843.

Until the end of World War I—and the establishment of the British Mandate for Palestine, the League of Nations provision that gave the British the power to administer parts of the defunct Ottoman Empire—the Yishuv's health care system operated mostly in a small public sector provided by charitable institutions and philanthropists. The Baron Edmond de Rothschild, a Jewish banker and philanthropist, established the first Jewish hospital in Jerusalem in 1854. The opening of three other religious hospitals in Jerusalem quickly followed. These were Bikur Holim in 1857, Misgav Ladach in 1879, and Shaarei Tzedek in 1902. All three were religious hospitals belonging to the different, isolated Jewish ethnic communities. The Vilna Gaon, the most outstanding anti-Hassidic rabbi, established the Bikur Holim organization. Then, with the help of Moses Montefiore, they established the Bikur Holim hospital, which provided services to the Ashkenazi community in Jerusalem. The Sefaradi community in Jerusalem set up the Misgav Ladach hospital with the help of rich Saloniki Jews. Finally, the German Jewish community established the Shaarei Tzedek hospital.

In the late nineteenth century, Jewish hospitals were also built in other cities and settlements (*moshavot*). In 1891, the Jaffa hospital (Shaarei Tzion) opened its doors. This hospital was different from the Jewish hospitals in Jerusalem. Those had been modeled on the structure of the old Yishuv, and were thus ethnically separated religious institutions. The Jaffa hospital, by contrast, was an institutional expression of mainstream Zionist ideology. It was Jewish, but rather than serving only one Jewish ethnic group, it served both Ashkenazim and Sephardim. Second, it was not a religious but a secular institution. Finally, it did not depend solely on charity from other countries. While charitable contributions were one of the sources that kept it alive, it was also financed by taxes paid by the community and by patients who paid for services according to their income. The Jaffa hospital, thus, presented the main characteristics of mainstream Zionism: a secular vision of the Jewish people as a national-cultural collective who shared a sense of republican solidarity.

The Baron Edmond de Rothschild funded two other Yishuv hospitals (Rishon le Tzion in 1889 and Zikhron Yaakov in 1890), which were located in what were called "the Baron settlements." Rothschild also financed the creation of open clinics and pharmacies in smaller settlements.

Because each Jewish community was a closed one, integration among the different hospitals into the beginnings of an organized health care system was impossible. Integration between the hospitals and primary care services belonging to different religious communities was even more difficult.

This fact reflected the major cleavages—based on country of origin, mother tongue, and religiosity—within the Jewish settler community. Those divisions generated different forms of communities within Palestinian and later Israeli society. If you arrived from Lithuania, Galizia, or Yemen you could be part of a community linked by country of origin. Orthodox Jews had their own communities with little contact with the secular immigrants.

But the main organizational axis was the one that combined ideology/party adherence and social class. This combination divided the Yishuv into four groups: (1) the Labor movement, (2) the religious bloc, (3) the revisionist movement, and (4) the petite bourgeoisie. These four groups developed institutions that covered the various aspects of everyday life within a settlers' society. Each of these groups developed institutions that provided services such as education, health care, cultural activities, and even sport activities. Among the four different blocs that constituted the Jewish community, the Labor movement became dominant in the early 1930s, when its chief political party, Mapai, reached power in the three main institutions: the Jewish Agency, the National Council, and the Histadrut.[2]

If curative medicine was poorly developed in the Yishuv's first years, preventive medicine was almost nonexistent. Up to 1912, the only preventive practices carried out were the quarantine, isolation, and disinfection procedures mentioned above. In 1912, Hadassah—an American women's Zionist organization—sent a group of nurses to Jerusalem to provide care for pregnant women and children. The nurses it recruited were Jewish women who came to Palestine to express solidarity with the Jewish settlement and contribute to the spread of Western scientific medicine. They shared the spirit of the Progressive era and believed in scientific management and public health as ways to advance human progress.[3] Hadassah considered pregnant women's and infants' hygiene and care, as well as health education, key areas in improving the health of the population as a whole. In 1916 Hadassah nurses opened the first "mother and child" clinic (Tachanat Em Veieled)—which provided health supervision and health education to pregnant women and infants. In 1919, it created a division of hygiene for school-aged children (Palti 1996, 81).

While a number of groups established hospitals and other services in the early twentieth century, Jewish workers in Palestine also began searching for solutions to the problem of health care provision. In 1911, the workers' federation of the Yehuda region set up a sick fund modeled on the German workers' sick funds—autonomous institutions, financed by the workers and their employers. These German sick funds provided medical care and "financial support in times of sickness and inability to work" (Frevert 1985). In Germany, workers who belonged to the sick funds could receive free medical treatment. The funds employed doctors and paid them an annual salary. The Jewish workers' sick funds adopted a similar model.

At the time of its creation, the Yehuda region's sick fund had 150 members. The Second Aliya[4] leader Berl Katzenelson defined its principles, stating that the sick fund would be based "upon the principle of mutual assistance of members," that "laborers and craftsmen who do manual work are accepted as members," and that "each member is obliged to actively participate in night watch at the bedside of a sick member, or else find a substitute in case he cannot meet this obligation himself" (quoted in Halevy, 1980:4–5). The Jewish workers organized the sick fund according to the principle that each "sick member will receive the assistance of a physician, medicine and lodging, and, when necessary, a place in a hospital" (quoted in Halevy 1980:4–5). After the establishment of this first sick fund, the workers' federations of the Shomron and Galilee regions established their own. There was an attempt to merge the three tiny sick funds into a common one. Instead, in 1919, they merged into two funds, each of them affiliated with one of the two largest workers' parties, Hapoel Hatzair and Ahdut Ha'avoda.

The Mandate Period

With the end of World War I, the Ottomans lost control of Palestine. With the Treaty of Sèvres (August 10, 1920), the Allied powers divided up the Ottoman Empire, giving Britain a "mandate" over Palestine. Over a period of several years, the boundaries of this territory shifted, covering what is now modern-day Israel, the West Bank, and Gaza Strip, and including and then excluding (in 1946) modern-day Jordan. During this period, the mainstream Zionist leaders who hoped to establish a permanent state in Palestine realized that to do this they would have to obtain "the support of the great powers for turning Palestine into a political center for Jewish people" and to form "an alliance with a great power" (Shlaim 2001:5). During the Mandate period (1920–1948), that power was Britain.

In Palestine during the Mandate period, the health care system continued to reproduce the earlier fragmentation of health care services. In 1920, for example, the British Mandate government established the public health department. This department was in charge of public health for both the Palestinian and the Jewish populations, and also managed hospitals and primary care facilities. By the end of 1922, the Mandate government ran ten hospitals as well as nineteen clinics and nine hospitals for contagious diseases in which both Arabs and Jews could get free yet minimal care. During World War II the government increased the amount spent on hospital facilities (but not the percentage of the budget spent on health), and in the 1940s the Mandate's services exceeded those offered by the missions. While in 1925 the Mandate government provided 14 percent of hospital beds, in 1944 it provided 33 percent. In 1945, besides the ten government hospitals for general medicine and infectious diseases, there were also three hospitals for mental illnesses.[5] The government also operated twenty-one outpatient clinics, all but one (in Tel Aviv) located in Arab or mixed cities.

Religious hospitals—both Jewish and Christian—based on principles of religious charity also increased in number under the Mandate. The British, German, French, and Italian missions established hospitals or clinics in Jerusalem, Nazareth, Ramallah, Nablus, Tiberias, Safed, Jaffa, Hebron, Gaza, and Haifa. By the end of the British Mandate there were twenty-two mission hospitals (eleven British, four French, four German, and three Italian). Jewish religious hospitals, such as Bikur Holim, Misgav Ladach, and Shaarei Tzedek were located mostly in Jerusalem.

Labor and Health Care

With the creation of the Histadrut (General Workers' Union) in 1920 as the unified organization of Jewish workers, the two sick funds, the Yehuda region and the Shomron and Galilee sick funds, merged into one organization, Kupat Holim Clalit (the General Sick Fund of the Workers of the Land of Israel), which remained the sick fund of the Histadrut until 1995.[6] The Histadrut was not only a trade union. Its goal was to be the nucleus of a workers' society, and it considered itself a central part of the Jewish national program to establish a Jewish national home in the land of Israel/Palestine.[7] As such, the trade union was only one—albeit central—branch of the organization. Other branches included a bank, a building company, cultural endeavors such as schools, a journal and a publishing company, and the sick fund, Kupat Holim Clalit. Every member of the union had to be a member of the sick fund, and every member of the sick fund a member of the union. Each member paid a uniform tax that would finance both the sick fund and the activities of the Histadrut's branches. Kupat Holim Clalit soon became the major health care provider of the prestate Jewish community. All the Jews that identified with the Labor movement were members of the Histadrut and thus received health care services from Kupat Holim Clalit.

The Hadassah Organization

The Hadassah organization continued to play a role during this period, establishing not only preventive health services but also hospitals that were the first incarnation of American-style medicine. In August 1918, this organization sent a health delegation—the American Zionist Medical Unit—to Palestine. The group included forty-four health care professionals: physicians, dentists, pharmacists, nurses, hygiene engineers, and health administrators. The Rothschild family transferred its Jerusalem hospital to

Hadassah, and in the following years Hadassah opened hospitals in all the urban centers of the Yishuv—Jaffa, Tel Aviv, Safed, Haifa, and Tiberias. The organization also opened dozens of clinics in rural settlements, which together with the small town clinics opened by the Rothschilds constituted the core of the ambulatory health care services of the Jewish Yishuv. While Hadassah was a Zionist organization, it provided health care to Palestinians as well as Jews.

In 1931, because of the Depression in the United States and the resulting difficulties in raising funds, Hadassah attempted to limit its involvement in the provision of health care services for the Jewish settlement in Palestine. To achieve this goal and disengage from providing medical care in the villages and agricultural areas, Hadassah founded the People's Fund, a sick fund in collaboration with the farmers' association (Hitachdut Haikarim). Members of the sick fund were independent farmers; that is, farmers who were not members of the kibbutz movement or the Moshavim (cooperative agricultural settlements).

Yishuv and Municipality Services

By the end of 1920 the National Council was constituted as the Jewish Yishuv's political executive. As a "government on the way," it was in charge of commissions that acted as facsimiles of what, in a state, would be considered government ministries. The health commission's role was to coordinate health activities in the Yishuv. In 1931, Hadassah transferred most of its hospitals to the Yishuv institutions and to the local communities. Tel Aviv's Hadassah hospital was transferred to the local municipality, and the hospital in Haifa to the Jewish community council of that city. Hadassah's Tiberias hospital became part of the National Council's Department of Health. In Jerusalem preventive health services were transferred to the municipality. This process continued with the transfer of the Tel Aviv preventive services (mother-and-child clinics and health supervision in schools) to the municipal authorities.

Other Sick Funds

Just as members of different Orthodox religious groups in fin de siècle Jerusalem would not have imagined going outside their religious community for hospital services, for secular Jews in the Yishuv, membership in sick funds was circumscribed by political commitments. Members of the Histadrut were members of Labor movement parties. They read the Histadrut newspaper *Davar;* they supported Hapoel, the Histadrut's soccer and basketball teams; if they had savings they put them at the Bank Hapoalim (the Workers' Bank); and, in the years before the establishment of the state in 1948, they sent their children to the worker movements' schools. They were also members of the Histadrut's sick fund, Kupat Holim Clalit, and saw doctors who worked for Clalit. The Clalit sick fund, however, provided services only for Histadrut members, who all belonged to the Labor movement. Since people from other political parties or with other political affiliations would not join the Histadrut, they could not receive health care services from the Clalit sick fund and had to search for other alternatives.

To address these problems, political parties opposed to Mapai, which was the dominant party in both the Histadrut and the National Council, created two new sick funds. In 1933 right-wing Revisionist Zionists founded the National Health Fund for those who could not obtain medical care from the Histadrut for political reasons.[8] The goal of this fund was to provide health care services to "each and every Jew whose income is not more than twenty Palestine pounds a month" (quoted in Halevy 1980:9). According to their right-wing nationalist ideology, they did not consider the Palestinian population as potential members.

The General Zionists (a national liberal party) founded their own sick fund, the General Zionist Sick Fund, in 1936. Its members were middle class, small-businessmen, and liberal professionals. The General Zionist party disappeared in 1965, and the sick fund changed its name to Kupat Holim Merkazit. In 1974 it merged with the already mentioned People's Fund to form Kupat Holim Meuhedet (United Sick Fund).

While the sick funds established in the 1920s and 1930s had a clear political affiliation, during the 1940s and 1950s physicians created several sick funds not related to political parties. The goals of these sick funds were to provide high-quality professional care and also to supply occupation to immigrant Jewish physicians, many of whom had come from Germany. The first among them—the Maccabi sick fund—was established in 1941 as a private business by unemployed immigrant physicians. In 1942, the Tel Aviv branch of the Israeli Medical Association (IMA) set up a sick fund, the Otzar Ha'rofim, and in 1950 the Haifa branch of the IMA opened the

Shiloah sick fund. These two funds merged in the early 1960s to form the Assaf sick fund, which amalgamated with Maccabi in 1975.

Prior to statehood in 1948, people belonged to a sick fund not because they preferred the services it provided or because they wanted to choose a particular doctor, but because the sick fund was part of a network of organizations that shaped individual and collective identities. The choice of a sick fund was, in the Yishuv years (1911–1948), part of a broader network that included party allegiances, social links, and cultural patterns, all merging in a defined pattern of ideological-political identities. Since in most sick funds (Maccabi was an exception) you could not choose your physicians or the hospital to which you were referred, choosing a sick fund was an expression of communal solidarity, not only for members but also for physicians, who were not allowed to work in private practice. So strong was the collectivist ideology that in 1946 "doctors at the Kupat Holim's Beilinson Hospital, many of them German born, signed a petition demanding they be allowed to live in their own houses outside the hospital grounds and to open private practices. They also insisted on 'the right to have a car and own paintings,' a violation of the austere values of the labor movement" (Segev 1991, 49).

The Israeli sick fund was, thus, not only part of a health care project but part of the labor movement's political project of building a Jewish national homeland. Although sick funds and other services were devoted to providing for the "common good"—this common good was understood as answering to the goals, aspirations, and culture of the secular, social democratic, Zionist, Ashkenazi Jews (Peled 1993; Kimmerling 2004). The early leaders of the Israeli state built and led through the political party Mapai, which in the 1960s adopted its current name: the Labor party.[9] Their particular brand of Zionism sought to combine the establishment of a strong Jewish homeland and flourishing institutional and economic life, with elements of workers' autonomous organization inspired by Austrian social democracy.[10]

The Early Years of Statehood (1948–1977)

With the establishment of the state of Israel in 1948, state institutions immediately replaced the Mandate government institutions and those run by the National Council at all levels: internal and external security, judiciary, planning, education, health, and so on. When Israel became a state, the new government did not create a central agency to coordinate its various health institutions. In 1948 the Kanev commission, a commission established by the government to prepare a plan to organize welfare services, proposed to implement a national health system similar to the British National Health System. Opposition from the IMA and the powerful Histadrut derailed this attempt. Physicians feared that the nationalization of the health care system would damage their professional autonomy as well as their income, and the Histadrut feared that a national health system would deprive the Histadrut of a tool to recruit members.

The lack of a national health care system, the weakness of the Ministry of Health, and the central role of the Histadrut in the early days of Israel's statehood made Kupat Holim Clalit (KHC) the central institution in health care. KHC insured more than 80 percent of the population and played a key role in the development of health care facilities. KHC delivered most ambulatory care and a significant proportion of hospital care, and it employed the highest number of health care workers (Greenberg 1983). In the 1950s, the Histadrut accepted Israeli Palestinians into its ranks. Thus KHC provided coverage to Israeli Palestinians and was the only sick fund that had clinics in the Israeli periphery, relatively far from the geographic and economic center, around Tel Aviv, where most Palestinian Arabs lived.

Mapai, the dominant party in Israel during its first three decades of statehood (1948–1978), controlled both the government coalition and the Histadrut, allowing KHC to receive important state subsidies (direct subsidies, subsidies for hospital beds, discounts, and so on). Mapai and other political groups associated with the Labor movement believed that health care had to be provided by the Labor movement's autonomous institutions and not by the state. The centrality of Kupat Holim Clalit allowed Mapai to strengthen its grip over its members and their families because, as noted above, every KHC member had to be a Histadrut member.[11]

The Ministry of Health (MOH), a department of the Israeli state government, was the other main institution in the Israeli health care system. The MOH was in charge of the planning and supervision of health care and of the provision of personal preventive services and psychiatric care. The MOH owned and ran several general and psychiatry hospitals. As mentioned above, however, the political weakness of the MOH vis-à-vis the Histadrut and KHC meant that, in practical terms, the KHC did most health planning.[12]

Municipalities, philanthropic and religious institutions, and secular NGOs also played an active role in the health care system through the ownership of hospitals, the organization of emergency care, the provision of special care, and the targeting of specific diseases. For example, the Tel Aviv municipality ran a hospital, religious institutions owned general hospitals in Jerusalem, the Hadassah organization ran hospitals in Jerusalem and Tel Aviv, and religious organizations ran hospitals in some Israeli Arab towns. Even though health care insurance was voluntary and all attempts to pass a law ensuring the right to health care failed, until the late 1970s the health care system was basically public and access to health care services did not require significant "out-of-pocket" payments. This was to change as the Likud took power in 1977 and with the neoliberalization process that began in the mid 1980s.

The Health Care System from the 1980s to the Present

Although a patient using the Israeli health care system today might find that it bears little resemblance to the system that existed during the British Mandate period and the early years of statehood, the system preserves key characteristics—namely, it remains mainly public and fragmented—that date back to the mid-twentieth century. Although neoliberal trends have eroded the system (as we shall see in chapter 2), it is still primarily public. It is also still fragmented, with little coordination among the various sectors and institutions. The MOH, moreover, still fails to effectively regulate the system. There is poor vertical and horizontal integration between the system's levels—preventive care, ambulatory care, and acute care (i.e., hospitalization).

In Israeli health care today, the following six separate sectors coexist without necessarily intersecting:

- preventive and environmental health services
- community services—psychiatric, geriatric, day care, and home care
- primary care services (provided mainly by the sick funds)

- specialists' ambulatory care in the community (provided mainly by the sick funds)
- specialists' ambulatory services in hospitals
- hospitalization (general hospitals, psychiatric hospitals, and chronic-care hospitals)
- supplementary services (e.g., first aid, emergency transport)

At each of these levels, dozens of institutions are responsible for providing health care services: the Ministry of Health (MOH), the sick funds, voluntary organizations (religious and nonreligious), city councils, nonprofit NGOs, and private institutions.

An external observer might think that the average Israeli citizen would get lost within this intricate network of institutions and levels of care. While in some cases (e.g., geriatric hospitalization and mental health services) this can happen, for most services the entrance point is the sick fund, through the family doctor, which greatly simplifies access. Through this gatekeeper, users reach all the curative services and hospitalization, and in some cases preventive care. Most patients are indifferent toward the kind of ownership or institutional affiliation of the various providers they meet. It is the sick fund that deals with the fragmentation of the system.

The MOH is responsible for planning, regulating, and supervising the health system as a whole, and it is also directly in charge of state-owned general and psychiatric hospitals, preventive services (mother-and-child clinics), and psychiatric services.[13] In its capacity as planner, the MOH is supposed to bring forward a global vision for the development of the health care system and to coordinate and integrate the various branches to implement this vision. As regulator, the MOH is responsible for ensuring that both the public and private sectors meet health standards set by the state The MOH supervises the provision of health care services (as well as the pharmaceutical sector, food production and processing, and environmental health). It is also responsible for health education and policy, licensing (medical and paramedical, as well as medicinal and cosmetic preparations), and promoting and updating health legislation.

Several factors, however, compromise the MOH's performance in this triple role. Because the Clalit sick fund (KHC) did most health care planning during Israel's first decades, the MOH has been historically weak. The independence of the sick funds made its role as regulator a difficult one. Its historical limitations have been exacerbated by the erosion of state welfare services in the neoliberal era. The MOH's roles as planner and regulator are also hampered by a conflict of interest in its roles as the owner and manager of many of the facilities it supervises and regulates.

As several commissions have stated, the MOH is so involved in the daily administration of health care provision that it cannot play an adequate role in planning, regulation, and control. According to Professor Arie Shirom, a member of the national committee that investigated the crisis of the health care system, the Ministry of Health is a main source of inefficiency: "(1) There is a serious problem concerning the setting of priorities, decision making and strategic thinking at the MOH (also because of the fact that the Ministry actually runs health services); (2) Salient deficiencies [exist] concerning planning and quality evaluation; (3) The MOH lacks control...over government budgets destined to health care" (Shirom 1993, 83). Thus, each sick fund or hospital undertakes its own planning, and central coordination is poor. Moreover, there are areas related to health under the jurisdiction of other ministries. The Ministry of Labor and Social Welfare oversees occupational health and provides custodial care for the mentally disabled. The Ministry of Agriculture is in charge of the control of animal diseases transmissible to humans. Municipal governments bear major responsibility for local water supply and sewage disposal, and some of them operate general hospitals and primary care.

The MOH budget reflects the complexity of its tasks. The budget for 2005 was New Israeli Shekels (NIS) 14.97 billion, of which 70.7 percent went to the financing of the health insurance law, 9.5 percent to mental health services, 7 percent for the treatment of prolonged diseases, 5.8 percent to support sick funds and hospitals, and 3.5 percent for public health and preventive medicine (Ministry of Finance [MOF] 2005).

The four Israeli nonprofit sick funds (Clalit, Maccabi, Meuhedet, and Leumit)—financed by a "health tax," state funds from the general budget, and member copayments—function like U.S. nonprofit health maintenance organizations (HMOs).[14] They provide a "basket" of services—including primary care, outpatient care, and hospitalization—to members.[15] As we shall see, membership in these sick funds and thus access to this basket of services is severely limited by the restrictive Israeli politics on citizenship. For example, migrant workers whose cheap labor has fueled economic growth in Israel since the early 1990s are largely excluded from access to the public health care system. Palestinians who are Israeli citizens are included in the public health care system but suffer from the under-development of services in their towns and villages.

The voluntary, nonprofit sector plays a relatively minor role in the Is-raeli health care system. It includes organizations such as Hadassah (which runs the Hadassah Medical Center); hospitals (e.g., mission hospitals and Shaarei Tzedek and Bikur Holim); the Magen David Adom agency (com-parable to the Red Cross) and others that provide emergency and am-bulance services; the Israeli Cancer Association, the Anti-Tuberculosis. League, and associations that care for handicapped children and the men-tally disabled. NGOs are engaged in many health-related areas, including patients' rights, human rights, the interests of patients suffering from spe-cific diseases, and family support.

Self-help organizations—for example, for parents of children suffering from conditions such as attention deficit disorder, for people with cystic fibrosis, and for those who suffer from multiple sclerosis—are part of this voluntary sector. These self-help groups are gathered under a common umbrella organization, Tzarkhanei Briut Tzvi (Health care consumers), which represents health care consumers.

City councils are in charge of part of the preventive care net, public health services and, in some cases, they also run hospitals. Some of the mother-and-child clinics are run by city councils, municipalities are in charge of public health services at the local level, and the Tel Aviv munici-pality runs the Ichilov Hospital. The analysis of each sector's share in the national health expenditure is a way of assessing the role of each sector in the Israeli health care system. The contribution of the major health care suppliers to health expenditure in 2006 was as follows:

- sick funds: 44 percent
- privately owned institutions: 23 percent
- MOH and local authorities: 21 percent
- nonprofit institutions: 12 percent

Looking at national health expenditure from a different angle, in 1995 40.6 percent of the national health budget went to hospitals and research, 34.5 percent to public clinics and preventive medicine, 11.1 percent to den-tal care, 4.5 percent to private physicians (the last two figures are estimates),

3.5 percent to medications bought by households, 1.1 percent to government administration, and 4.7 percent to fixed capital formation (Central Bureau of Statistics [CBS] 2007).

Health Care System Today

Preventive Medicine

Preventive care consists mainly of personal preventive services such as the mother-and-child clinics and medical screening in elementary schools. The mother-and-child clinics care for women during pregnancy and undertake immunizations and the monitoring of healthy babies. Other preventive services (such as occupational health) are underdeveloped in Israel (Shirom 1993). The MOH provides most preventive care, while a few mother-and-child clinics are operated by the sick funds—mainly KHC—and the municipalities. In 1995, out of a total of 1,000 family health clinics, some 650 belonged to the MOH and 300 to KHC, while the family health clinics in Jerusalem and Tel Aviv belonged to the municipalities.

Preventive services are underfunded when compared with other areas of the health system. Only 2 percent of the national health expenditure is allotted to such services, and almost half of this expenditure is financed by its users.[16] Until 1995, the MOH and the city councils provided school-age preventive services. Since then, and as part of the trend toward privatization, these services have been outsourced to a private subcontractor supervised by the MOH (Palti 1996).

Primary Care

Most, if not all, primary care is provided by the four sick funds. Primary care includes all those activities (preventive, diagnostic, curative, palliative, counseling, and rehabilitating) performed by a health care provider (or providers) who acts as a first point of consultation. As is the case with the majority of services, primary care is not equally distributed between center and periphery. In Israel, periphery is not only a geographic concept but also a social one. The southern area is much poorer than Gush Dan, the central area (which includes cities such as Tel Aviv, Ramat Gan,

Givatayim, Raanana, and Kfar Saba). While there is a "social periphery" (population that resides in the central area but who are excluded from access to services and commodities because of their low socioeconomic status) within those cities, in general terms the geographic periphery includes poorer and more excluded social groups. These groups include not only the Arabs, Bedouins, and migrant workers about which we will learn more in the next chapters but also Ethiopian Jews, Jewish immigrants from Arab countries ("Mizrahim"), and immigrants from the former republics of the Soviet Union.

Many of these Jews who immigrated to Israel after World War II did not fit the secular, Eurocentric Ashkenazi elite's conception of who should and should not flock to Israel. Jews who emigrated from Arab countries such as Yemen, Morocco, Tunisia, and Iraq were settled in agricultural settlements or development towns in the geographic periphery and mostly employed in blue-collar jobs. Israeli Arabs, with the exception of those living in Jaffa and Haifa, also tend to live in peripheral towns and villages and belong, by and large, to the lower socioeconomic strata. This processes built a tiered periphery where geography, ethnicity, and class converge.

As a consequence of the unequal distribution of material resources and political power, all services—including health care—are less developed in the geographic periphery. Health indicators reflect socioeconomic disparity as well as differences in the quantity and quality of health care services. In 1994, the Tel Aviv district had the highest concentration of physicians (687 per 100,000), followed by Haifa (598.7), Petach Tikva, (555.4), Jerusalem (485.4), Safed (482.8), and Rehovot (469.5). The lowest concentrations of physicians were in the Kinneret and Ramla districts (176.4 and 197.5 respectively) (B. Swirski et al. 1998). The number of hospital beds per 1,000 people is also significantly higher in the Tel Aviv and Haifa regions (2.7) than in the southern region (1.5). In the northern and southern regions, mortality rates are higher than the national average, and the highest infant mortality rate is in the southern Beer Sheva district. While these differences have existed for decades, they have recently generated growing social opposition. For example, in 2007 a group of women from the southern city of Beer Sheva organized under the name "The Beer Sheva Groups: Equality in Health." With the support of Physicians for Human Rights, they are struggling against the differences in access to health care. Their first goal is to make public all available data on differences in the quantity and quality of health care services because they believe that public knowledge is the first step toward modifying the current situation.

Secondary Care

Secondary care, or specialty medicine, is supplied by the sick funds, the MOH, and the municipalities (specialists' clinics in hospitals). Lack of co-ordination among the various subsystems in this area translates into ineffi-ciency. Fragmentation and lack of integration result in duplications, poor coordination between specialists and primary care physicians, reduced qual-ity control of care, and inadequate distribution of specialists. Hospitals run outpatient specialists' clinics. The sick funds, in order to cut referral costs, have opened, since the late 1980s, their own specialists' clinics. The irony is that the same physicians sometimes work at both clinics: They are at the hospital until the early afternoon and at the sick funds' clinics in the eve-ning. While in the last few years the sick funds have exerted better con-trol over referrals, there are still patients who are followed by two different cardiologists or ophthalmologists, one at the sick fund and a second one at the hospital. The MOH is a weak regulator and thus there is no mid-range planning to adapt the number of specialists to the population needs. Thus there is a surplus of certain specialists, such as ophthalmologists and gyne-cologists, and a deficit of others, such as geriatricians and anesthesiologists.

Hospitalization

Tertiary care—that is, hospitalization—is provided by the MOH (45 percent of general beds and most mental services), the sick funds (primarily Cla-lit), voluntary organizations, municipalities, and the private sector. In Israel there are 369 hospitals: 300 for chronic care (including nursing wards in old-age homes and kibbutzim), 47 for general care, 20 for psychiatric care, and 2 rehabilitation hospitals. Of these 369 hospitals, 165 are owned by t orga-nizations other than governmental ones or the sick funds, 146 by nonprofit organizations, 25 belong to the MOH, 24 to the sick funds (13 to Clalit, 6 to Maccabi, and 5 to Meuhedet), 7 to the missions, and 2 to city councils.

Out of a total of 41,618 hospital beds, 11,164 belong to the MOH, 5,443 to the Clalit sick fund, and 1,455 to the city councils; 12,687 are private, 9,709 nonprofit, 646 belong to the missions, 248 to the Maccabi sick fund, and

266 to the Meuhedet sick fund. The percentage of utilization is very high and the turnover fast, but the number of hospitalization days per 1,000 inhabitants is high in international terms. In 1995, this figure was 2,041 days per 1,000 people (compared with 1,230 days per 1,000 population in 1993 in the Organization for Economic Cooperation and Development [OECD] countries) (B. Swirski et al. 1998). The Israeli figure is remarkably high if we take into account that the country's population is younger than the OECD population. Although it is not easy to explain the reason for the high number of hospitalization days, there are two important contributing factors: First, in the 1960s and 1970s the primary care system was less developed and had a poorer image than hospitals, and the public preferred to be referred to the latter. Second, the MOH remunerates hospitals based on the cost of hospitalization day, creating a financial incentive to increase hospitalizations.

In sum, while the Israeli health care system is highly developed, technologically advanced, and rich in human resources, it lacks both vertical and horizontal integration and coordination. Each institution formulates its own strategies, and there is very little central planning.

Despite these shortcomings, however, the system has achieved very good results. Israel's health indicators are similar to those of developed countries, whether we consider infant mortality and life expectancy or human and material resources.

Life expectancy in Israel was 77.6 for men and 81.8 for women in 2003, higher than in the United States. Men's life expectancy in Israel is among the highest in the world, while women's life expectancy is similar to the average in developed countries. There is no single explanation for this finding, and no epidemiological studies have been carried out to account for it.[17] The anthropologist Susan Sered has explained the small gap in life expectancy as the result of the ways in which the particular characteristics of Israel's patriarchy (the state support of maternity, the normalization of the military, and the institutional role of rabbis) contribute to make women sick (Sered 2000).

Morbidity and infant mortality indicators are also similar to those of the rich countries. The main causes of death (cancer and cardiovascular disease) coincide with those of Western European countries. The standardized death rate (SDR) for cardiovascular diseases between the ages of 0 and 64 is close to the European Union (EU) average (data from 1992), and the SDR for cancer for the same age group is low in comparison with the EU. Regarding infant mortality, infant deaths are caused by congenital malformations (25%), perinatal mortality (50%), and other or unspecified causes (20%). Worldwide, mortality and morbidity data of ethnic or religious minorities and the poor are worse than average. Israel is no exception. Life expectancy is lower among Israeli Arabs than among Israeli Jews, and infant mortality is almost double (discussed in chapter 3). Mortality rates are higher in those localities and towns with poorer socioeconomic indicators.

Resource availability and utilization in the Israeli health care system is also similar to the EU countries. Israel per capita spending on health care is similar to that of the EU countries. Health expenditure measured as a percentage of the gross domestic product (GDP) is also similar to that of OECD countries. In 1994, before the National Health Insurance law came into effect, Israel spent 8.9 percent of its GDP on health.[18] Health expenditure as percentage of the GDP reached its highest level in 2002 (9.3%) and went down in 2004 to 8.1 percent, and to 7.8 percent in 2006.

Human resources are abundant, since Israel has a large supply of health care professionals. The Israeli health care system is an intensive manpower employer. In 2003 there were 156,900 people employed in the system (some 6% of the total working population) (CBS 2005). Of these, 30 percent were nurses, 12 percent physicians, and 58 percent other professionals.[19] In 1993, the number of licensed physicians was estimated at 4.6 per 1,000, compared with the OECD average of 2.5 practicing physicians per 1,000 (MOH 1998). World Health Organization (WHO) data shows that in 1993, Israel had a total of 24,100 physicians (the aforementioned 4.6 per 1,000), 6,886 dentists (1.3 per 1,000), and 37,772 nurses (6.7 per 100,000 in 1995). Israel has one of the highest per-capita proportions of physicians—1 physician per 340 inhabitants in 1995. In terms of comparison, at that time in the United States, there were 2.2 physicians per 1,000 people and in France 3.2.

If we take into account immigrant physicians from the former USSR, the proportion of physicians is even higher, 1 physician for every 210–220 inhabitants, more than 4 per 1,000 population. In the 1990s, a new wave of immigrants—Jews migrating from the former Soviet Union—entered Israel. Many of these émigrés were physicians, adding considerably to the rate of physicians and leading to the modification of licensing norms. Before the massive Soviet immigration, Jewish physicians from Europe,

America, Latin America, and even some from the Soviet Union were allowed to practice medicine in Israel without taking any exams at all. With the mass influx of Soviet physicians that began in 1989, the MOH changed its rules and required a licensing examination to vet physicians' competence and education.

In 1992, there were 2.5 general hospital beds per 1,000 inhabitants (while the United Kingdom had 2.2 beds for 1,000 persons, the United States 3.5, the Netherlands 4.2, and Italy 5.5); in 2003, this figure went down to 2.1. The mean bed utilization in 1992 was 91.7 percent, and 98.3 percent for general care beds. The median length of stay in general hospitals in 2004 was 4.6 days (which is low when compared with the EU). The number of hospitalizations per 1,000 inhabitants is high by EU standards—in 1997 there were 198 hospitalizations per 1,000 inhabitants (20.4% for cardiovascular diseases, 11.5% for respiratory diseases, 9.6% for intoxications and trauma, 7% for malignancies, and 3.5% for infectious diseases).

Primary care utilization has decreased between the 1980s and the 1990s. Data cited by J. Shuval for 1990 shows 12.3 physician contacts per year (Shuval 1992). Utilization data from the CBS for 1998 shows an average of 7.1 visits per year to a family practitioner, and another 2.6 visits per year to dentists. In 2004 the average number of visits to a family doctor was 4.7 a year and to a dentist 1.5 (CBS 1998, 1998b, 2006). In 1993, 83 percent of the most recent visits to a general practitioner or family doctor were made to sick fund clinics, 12 percent to private clinics, and 35 percent to hospital outpatient clinics or emergency rooms. Regarding visits to specialists, 61 percent took place at sick fund clinics, 21 percent at hospital outpatient clinics or emergency rooms, and 16 percent at private clinics (from Israeli data to the UN Commission on Social Rights). Concerning the use of preventive services, 85 percent of Jewish children and 81 percent of Arab children had their immunization schedule completed (B. Swirski et al. 1998). These figures are high when compared with other countries and reflect the emphasis the MOH gave to immunizations until recently. Lately, as a consequence of the budget constraints resulting from neoliberal policies, the Israeli immunization schedule has not been updated as in other industrialized countries and does not include immunizations against pneumococcal infections in children, rotavirus, and papilloma virus.

Israel's health indicators and the characteristics of its health care system are those of a developed country. The expenditure in health, the ways of financing the system, and the extension of the public system are also similar to those of the majority of developed countries. National health expenditure in Israel in 2004 was about $11.2 billion (NIS 44,827 billion), which represents 8.1 percent of the GDP, and per-capita expenditure of about $1,720 (NIS 6800). As mentioned earlier, Israel's health care system is a single-payer system. Public health services are financed by (1) a health tax (4.8% of income) collected by the National Insurance Institute and distributed among the four sick funds by a corrected capitation formula, (2) the MOH budget, and (3) copayments for some services (e.g., medical imaging, specialist ambulatory services, private dental care).[20]

In 1999, 72.9 percent of the national health expenditure was financed by the government and local authorities, and 27.1 percent by households (this data does not include the health tax; it only includes complementary and private insurance and out-of-pocket expenditure). In 1998 (before the implementation of copayment for specialist services in KHC), the participation of the government and local authorities in the financing of national health expenditure went down to 69 percent, and household participation went up to 29 percent (CBS 1999).[21]

The Health Care System and the Reproduction of Oppression and Exclusion

While Israel's health indicators represent a remarkable accomplishment for its health care system, they also reveal serious patterns of inequality. In fact, Israeli statistics look so positive because they do not measure the health status of the Palestinians in the Occupied Territories. In the aftermath of the 1967 war, Palestinians in the Occupied Territories became the outermost circle of exclusion, denied even liberal rights. The poor health of the Palestinians in the OPT is a direct result of forty years of Israeli occupation. Moreover, the health status of the Israeli Palestinians is poorer than the health status of Israeli Jews.

The health status of the Israeli Arabs, those Palestinians who after the 1948 war remained within Israel and became Israeli citizens, is a result of geographic segregation; the aforementioned convergence of geography, class, and ethnicity; and the exclusionary nature of Israeli citizenship.

Citizenship in Israel has been primarily defined in terms of the republican conception of citizenship (Shafir and Peled 2002).[22] In Israel, a hierarchy was constructed in which Ashkenazi Jews (Jews who emigrated from European countries, mostly Russia and Poland)—the state-building elite—were at the top, Mizrahi Jews (Jews who emigrated mostly from Arab countries) occupied a lower position, and Palestinians who are Israeli citizens occupied the lowest ones. Following the 1967 war, the outer circle was occupied by Palestinians residing in the Occupied Territories, who were also denied liberal and political rights. Only Jews participate in deciding the country's common goals, policies, and future direction. All of the state's symbols—its flag, its national anthem—are exclusively Jewish. The dominance of Jewish Israelis is not a matter of law but a result of the unequal distribution of power between the two national groups. Legally, Israeli Palestinians enjoy full citizenship rights. They can vote and be elected to Parliament. A Palestinian can even be legally elected as Prime Minister. In reality, however, there has never been a government elected in Israel in which a Palestinian party has even been part of the governing coalition.

Israeli Palestinians enjoy "negative" personal and formal political rights. They have freedom of religion, congregation, and expression, the right to due process, freedom of movement, the right to elect and be elected.[23] They are, however, discriminated against when it comes to budgetary allocations—particularly those affecting the development of their towns and villages—and land allocation. Arab settlements confront difficulties when they apply for permits for their expansion. Moreover, a significant percentage of the public land in Israel is owned by the National Jewish Fund, and, until recently, when the Supreme Court changed this, Israeli Arabs could not buy any land owned by the National Jewish Fund. Communities built on these lands were for Jews only.

In true republican manner, military service is considered an essential citizen virtue; this cultural attitude influences allocation of resources. Since they are part of the Palestinian people and the Arab nation, Israeli Palestinians do not serve in the military. Some ultra-orthodox Jews refuse to serve in the Army for theological reasons and do not consider themselves part of the Zionist community. Unlike the Israeli Arabs, ultra-orthodox Jews are not discriminated against when it comes to allocation of financial resources, demonstrating that ethnonational criteria are more important than republican ones (Shafir and Peled 2002).

Palestinians living in the Occupied Territories are not Israeli citizens and do not enjoy the benefits of citizenship. They cannot immigrate to Israel. They do not have access to Israel's social services, and, as we will see in chapter 5, they have only limited access to the health care system.

Health indicators in the OPT are much worse than in Israel, a reflection on these policies and political decisions. Life expectancy in the OPT is 72.6 (men 71.1, women 74.1). Infant mortality is 20.1 per 1,000 live births, and for children under five, the mortality rate is 23.8 (WHO 2004).

Within Israel, the health indicators of Israel's Palestinian citizens—which are included in health statistics—are worse than those of the Jewish population. Infant mortality is almost double for Palestinians who are Israeli citizens than for Jewish Israeli citizens (8.3 per 1,000 live births vs. 3.6 per 1,000 live births in 2004). Infant mortality also reflects the differences between Jews and Palestinians who are Israeli citizens. While infant mortality rates are decreasing for both groups, the difference between them is growing. Total infant mortality in 2003 was 4.9 per 1,000 live births. Infant mortality among Jews went down from 7.6 per 1,000 in 1990 to 3.6 per 1,000 in 2003 (a decline of 53%). For the same years, the infant mortality rate among Palestinians dropped from 14.6 percent in 1990 to 8.3 percent in 2003 (a 43% decline).[24] The relative risk ratio of Arabs compared with that of Jews is higher in the post-neonatal period (3.4 times higher for Israeli Arabs in 1990–1993), underlining the effect of socioeconomic factors.

Israeli Arabs' life expectancy is also lower. Life expectancy was 78.1 for Jewish men and 82.2 for Jewish women, while it was 74.9 for Arab men and 78.2 for Arab women (CBS 2005).[25] Life expectancy at sixty years old in 1995–1999 was 20.2 for men and 22.6 years for women, but within this group, too, there were differences between Jews and Arabs (20.3/19.8 for men and 22.8/21.1 for women) (CBS 2005). When people are asked to assess their own health, the same inequality between Jewish and Palestinian citizens appears. Among Palestinian Israelis, 10 percent report poor health, compared with 5 percent among Jewish citizens.

Inequality also has a geographic dimension. Overall mortality rates per 100,000 are significantly higher for most age groups in the Negev region, in the south of Israel, compared with the rest of the country. Mortality figures for infections, chronic ischemic heart disease, and cerebrovascular disease are higher in the Negev than in the rest of the country (Tulchinsky and Ginsberg 1996). Despite the high ratio of physicians per inhabitants, the geographic distribution of physicians is uneven. In 1994, the Tel Aviv district had more than 1,000 physicians per 100,000 residents, while the Golan and Ramleh districts had slightly more than 200 physicians per 100,000 residents (CBS 1999).

Health indicators reflect not only status inequality but also economic inequality. People in the lowest socioeconomic status (SES) quintile have less access to services (Berg et al. 2002). Moreover, when people are asked about their own health, the poor and less educated report more health problems. Among those earning less that 2,000 NIS ($570) per capita, 10.2 percent report poor health, compared with 2.3 percent among people earning more that 4,000 NIS ($1140) per capita. Among people who did not finish high school, 16.3 percent report poor health, compared with 2.4 percent among those with an academic degree.

Poorer and minority groups visit doctors more often than well-to-do Jewish Israelis. Data shows that among adults aged eighteen and up, the number of visits to a physician decreases as the level of education increases (CBS 1999). In addition, people who are unemployed visit physicians twice as much as those with jobs. Some might argue that the unemployed have more free time to explain this phenomenon. Visits to physicians, however, usually reflect poor health rather than a lack of occupation or something to do. Both Shuval's (1992) and CBS (1993) data document that women visited doctors more often than men in all age groups, except for girls under five years old and those aged 75 and over.

Differences in health status generally reflect inequality in the society as a whole and are not solely the result of inequalities in access to health care. However, the unequal distribution of health care resources deepens those differences. Resources are unevenly distributed among different social groups and between center and periphery. Even though there is a national health insurance law that ensures health care (a common health-services basket) for every citizen or permanent resident,[26] inequalities still persist. The geographic distribution of resources is unequal both in quantity and quality of services and personnel (Shuval 1992, 293). As Swirski et al. point out, "cities and suburban communities have more and better services than peripheral communities, Jews have more than Arabs and veteran communities more than development towns" (B. Swirski et al. 1998, 8).[27] Private care, moreover, selectively restricts access to care. This limiting effect is obvious when we compare the previous figures to data on dental health, which is private in Israel. Only 41 percent of children ages five and six have no cavities at all, and 75 percent of Israelis have no regular dental checkup (B. Swirski et al. 1998).

Although the Israeli health care system is rich in human and financial resources and has produced some remarkable results, even its Jewish citizens suffer from its fragmentation and lack of coordination. Even more troubling is that its structure and outcomes reflect the cleavages in Israeli society—Jewish citizens get better services and enjoy better health indicators. As we saw before, the infant mortality rate and the under-five-year child mortality rate for Arab citizens is double that of Jewish citizens. Age-standardized rates of death from all causes combined are higher for Arabs than for Jews, and age-standardized rates of death from external causes (mostly accidents) are 30 percent higher (slightly lower for Arab women) (B. Swirski et al. 1998).[28] Even though most of the differences in health status are related to the socioeconomic gap, the few available data show that primary care and preventive services are less developed in Arab towns and villages (B. Swirski et al. 1998).

The Israeli health care system reproduces the inequalities generated by the unequal distribution of power and resources. As we will see in chapter 2, the neoliberalization of Israeli society deepens these inequalities because it creates income- and class-dependent obstacles to health care access, even among Jewish Israelis.

2

The "Neoliberalization" of the Israeli Health Care System

We arrived at the meeting with the new regional director of Kupat Holim Clalit's (KHC) Tel Aviv area with apprehension. He had summoned the directors of all KHC clinics to a meeting to explain his program, and we did not know what to expect. In 1993 KHC was going through a severe crisis. There had been a major reorganization of the sick fund. Many young patients were leaving KHC for smaller sick funds, and many medications were unavailable at KHC's pharmacies. As a way to cope with the crisis, Prime Minister Rabin forced the Histadrut (General Workers' Union) to designate a new CEO for Kupat Holim. Rabin's choice was Avigdor Kaplan, who was the CEO of the U.S. branch of the Israeli Aerospace Industries.

Kaplan, who had no experience in health care, approached KHC as another business enterprise. He reduced the number of geographic sections by half and appointed new regional directors. The clinic where I worked since 1990 and whose director I was since 1991 belonged to the Jaffa district (which included not only Jaffa but also the cities Bat Yam and Holon). Now it was to be merged with the Tel Aviv district.

The meeting was not a pleasant one. The new regional director reviewed the highlights of the crisis facing KHC and informed us of management's plan to deal with it. While the fundamental structural cause of the crisis was the change in the state's approach to the financing of the health care system, management believed its solution was the adoption of an organizational culture more similar to that of the business sector. The new director stressed the need to limit the influence of the professional organizations and trade unions in managerial decisions. He told us we must cut costs wherever possible and begin to think about our patients as "clients." Finally, he emphasized the need to decentralize responsibility (though not strategic planning) to the "front-line units—that is, the primary care clinics. For the next years, he said, KHC would put this new organizational vision into practice.

My personal experience reflects the transition that Israeli society has made since the mid-1980s as it has moved from a Keynesian socioeconomic model—based on state intervention, a strong public sector, agreements among between the state, employers, and trade unions, and a relatively strong welfare state—to the neoliberal socioeconomic model (Filc 2004; Ram 2007). At KHC, patients and their caregivers were—on a daily basis— coping with the results of the erosion of universal public welfare institutions as they discovered what it means when the "discipline of the market" begins to distribute resources and controls access to services. Patients and caregivers learned what happens when the institutions they work for and depend on shift priorities—moving away from the goal of distribution according to needs (even if those needs were mediated by political processes and influences). This shift had three main goals: (1) reducing public spending to free resources for the accumulation of capital, (2) opening new fields of investment, and (3) disciplining the labor force (Agger 1985; Esping Anderssen 1990).

Since the health care system represents a significant part of public spending and a tempting field for investment, the privatization of health care is central to this process. In the last three decades, patients and those who care for them in welfare states around the world have experienced similar problems as their societies began to reform their health care systems and included privatization of services and/or the incorporation of market mechanisms into public health care systems. The need to control costs in the field of health care is also related to the exponential increase in health expenditure due to the aging population and to the dominance of a hi-tech approach to health care, based on the constant development of new expensive technologies.

In Israel the privatization of the health care system included three aspects. The first one was the privatization of the financing of health care service. The second was the privatization of ownership of health care facilities. The last was the incorporation into a public health care system of a managerial culture (one used to produce goods and services in the business sector), adapted, however maladroitly, to provide services to the sick and vulnerable.

In Israel, this transformation was not a smooth or unambivalent one. Mirroring a broader debate about the goal of government and public life, the corporatization of the Israeli health care system was full of contradictions. Along with a partial shift from public to private financing of health care and the increase in private ownership of health care facilities, the Knesset (the Israeli parliament) in 1994 legislated a National Health Insurance (NHI) law that ensured universal health care and emphasized equality of access and quality of treatment. Even this law was unable to fully temper the neoliberal dynamic, and only two years after the legislation of the NHI law the privatization process deepened, increasing inequality and exclusion.

Privatization of Financing

The first step in the neoliberalization of health care in Israel was the deliberate decision to politically shift the financing of the health care system from the state to private citizens. The goal of this shift was to cut public expenditure in order to lower taxes, thus freeing resources for the process of capital accumulation. In Israel as elsewhere, public financing is the institutional expression of a communal commitment: The healthier, younger, and better off subsidize the older, sicker, and poorer population. As Paul Farmer, a physician and medical anthropologist, founder of Partners in Health, a nonprofit NGO providing care for the poor in countries such as Haiti, Lesotho, and Malawi, has expressed it, "I would argue that a social justice approach should be central to medicine and utilized to be central to public health. This could be very simple: the well should take care of the sick." The privatization of financing, on the other hand, means that those who are older (who need more health care services than the young) and sicker carry the weight of financing, making access to services dependent on income. This inevitably makes it much harder for poorer people to get health care services.

Until the legislation of the NHI law, the funding of health care in Israel was highly pluralistic (Bin Nun and Chinitz, 1993), with funds coming directly from the government via general taxes, from an earmarked tax paid by employers, and from public health insurance. Private financing was also bifurcated with funds coming from private insurance and "out-of-pocket" payments (paid directly upon receiving a service such as visits to a private doctor, the purchase of medicines, or payment for medical equipment).

Government monies financed preventive medicine, government hospitals, and psychiatric services. Moreover, until the late 1970s, the government covered KHC's deficits. Since KHC provided health care services for the oldest and poorest and was the only sick fund that provided services to the entire periphery, it was always running budget deficits. Until the late 1970s the Labor party dominated both the government coalition and the Histadrut's leadership, and thus it was able to subsidize KHC's deficit and had a political interest in doing so.

The sick funds were financed from various sources, the largest source being an employer-paid, earmarked tax that amounted to about 5 percent of taxable income, up to an income ceiling. Until 1991, this tax was distributed to the funds on the basis of a formula that gave a weight of 75 percent to the income of a fund's member and 25 percent to the size of a fund's enrollment. The second source was a membership fee, which amounted to 4.8 percent of the member's wage. This membership fee was paid directly to each sick fund. Someone earning 2,000 dollars a month would pay about 100 dollars a month as a membership fee and would have to pay more if he or she (or their children) had to visit a dentist or as copayments for some drugs.

In the case of KHC, the membership fee paid not only for health care services but for all the activity of the Histadrut (75% of the fee funded KHC and 25% all the other services provided by the union). Since the income of the sick funds depended on their members' income, the funds had an incentive to appeal to the wealthier sector of the population. Sick funds were also financed by copayments, mostly for prescription drugs. Some of the small sick funds also charged small copayments for primary care and community specialists.

To fight the three-digit inflation in the early 1980s, the Israeli national unity government, a coalition of the Labor and the Likud parties formed after the 1984 elections, adopted an economic plan designed by neoliberal economists and strongly backed by U.S. Secretary of State George Schultz and by several American academics such as Stanley Fisher.[1] There were two reasons for the U.S. interest in backing the plan. First, the U.S. State Department was worried that hyperinflation would destabilize the Israeli government, which in those years was already the United States' main ally in the region. Second, the United States was invested in promoting worldwide neoliberal reforms (the Washington Consensus). The close geopolitical relationship with the United States, along with the broader Americanization of Israeli society, had a central influence on the neoliberalization of the Israeli economy in general and of the health care system in particular. Schultz and Fisher's influence on the Israeli economy reflected the shift in geopolitical alliances that occurred in Israel after statehood. When Israel fought for an independent state in the war of 1948 and sought international support for that state, the Soviet Union (USSR) was their biggest supporter. The intervention of Andrei Gromyko, the Soviet ambassador to the United Nations, was central to the 1947 resolution on the partition of Palestine. Moreover, although the United States announced its de facto recognition of the new Israeli state on May 14, 1948, the USSR outdid the United States by declaring its de jure recognition two days later (Pappe 2004). The United States had a distinctly hands-off attitude toward Israel. On several occasions, for example, the Eisenhower administration refused appeals from Prime Minister Ben Gurion to sell Israel weapons.

Not so the Soviet Union. As Tom Segev has written in his study of the Americanization of Israeli society, *Elvis in Jerusalem,* "Communist bloc countries had sold Israel some of its arms during the War of Independence. Moscow was the capital of world socialism and some of the parties in Ben-Gurion's coalition,...considered themselves part of the socialist world" (Segev 2001, 55).

The United States was not pleased with this alliance and began trying to influence Israel through cultural propaganda (Segev 2001). In the 1950s, and as the Cold War deepened, Ben Gurion made a strategic decision to tie Israel's future to the Western bloc. During the Korean War, smaller nations like Israel were asked to choose between the USSR and the U.S.–led Western bloc. Israel's relationship with the USSR began to fray as the Soviet Union increasingly supplied arms and support to the Arab countries.

Change accelerated in the early 1960s. The first indication of a change in the U.S. approach to Israel was the Kennedy administration's decision—as part of the Pentagon's approach to the Cold War and as a result of "mounting internal pressure"—to sell weapons to Israel (Gazit 2000). The Johnson administration not only continued this approach but considered Israel as a strategic asset. At the same time, the USSR became the Arab world's main supporter and provider of weapons. Forbidding Jews to leave the country became another element of tension. The tension reached its peak after the 1967 war, when the USSR broke its diplomatic relationship with Israel.

The 1967 war cemented Israel's dependence on the United States, which has deepened since (Little 1993). As a consequence of the war and the strengthening of the economic and military dependence on the United States, the military-industrial complex strengthened, becoming the most dynamic sector of the Israeli economy. As Israel's dependence on U.S. military aid increased,[2] the "American world view" increasingly permeated Israeli society, its economy, its political culture, its popular culture, and its dreams (Ram 2007). American opposition to taxes and to public sector spending, the power of the Labor movement and labor unions, the virtues of the private sector, and the almost religious conviction that the market can do no wrong began to permeate Israeli politics and consciousness.

In Israel, one of the first political expressions of this process was the role that the American economist Milton Friedman played as assessor of Menahem Begin's government when the Likud party reached power in 1977.[3] By the time the leaders of the national unity government—the Labor party's Shimon Peres as prime minister, Likud's Yitzhak Shamir as foreign minister, and Likud's Yitzhak Modai as minister of finance—took office in 1984, they had integrated U.S. neoliberal ideas into their economic program. Their economic plan included a significant decrease in real wages and a deep cut in government spending (including security and welfare). As a consequence, the government's share in the financing of health care services decreased from 34 percent of total health care expenditure in the late 1970s to 21.6 percent in the 1990s. Not surprising, the government also stopped covering the KHC's deficit (Chernichovsky 1991).

Thus, during the second half of the 1980s, KHC, the largest and most powerful sick fund in Israel, faced a severe financial crisis. It had trouble paying providers and owed money to state-owned hospitals. Patients had to wait for weeks to see specialists and for several months for elective surgical procedures. In addition, KHC had great difficulty paying for and thus supplying more expensive prescription drugs.

The budget cuts in the mid- and late 1980s deeply modified the financing of the national health care. In 1980 the government financed 60 percent of the national health expenditure, sick fund membership fees covered 12 percent, and citizens paid 19 percent directly out of their pockets. In 1989, only nine years later, the government's share had decreased to 47 percent, members' fees had increased to 20 percent, and direct, out-of-pocket payments had jumped to 28 percent of the national health expenditure (almost a 50% increase!).

As a consequence of the reduction in public financing, the growth rate of the real total national expenditure on health declined in the 1980s, from 6.48 percent to 2.72 percent, while the per-capita growth rate fell from 3.9 to 1.05. Government investment in health also declined (Chernichovsky 1991). The most striking change between the 1970s and the 1980s was the drop in the government's share in health care financing, which fell from 45 percent to 21 percent due to the decline in the use of general taxation to finance health services. With the government funding fewer services, patients had to pay up front to gain access to the system. And indeed, out-of-pocket household expenditure at point of service increased from 19 percent of the total health care expenditure in 1980 to 28 percent in 1989 (Bin Nun and Chinitz 1993) and remained high during the early 1990s.

The reduction of government spending on health care caused a serious financial strain on the public health care system, and especially on KHC (Chernichovsky 1991; Shirom 1993). Because of the case- and age-mix of its members, KHC was extremely dependent on government financing.[4] Its financial situation worsened during most of the 1980s, fueling the development of a multitiered health care system. Faced with long lines and poorer care, the young, healthy, upper-middle-class population chose to transfer to the small sick funds, which invested more per capita and rejected elderly patients and those suffering from chronic conditions. Through this practice of "cream-skimming," these smaller sick funds succeeded in enrolling younger, healthier, and more affluent members.

While KHC deficits were financed by general revenues, the quality and types of service were similar in all the sick funds. Yet as KHC plunged into a financial crisis, the gap in per capita expenditure among the different sick funds increased. The crisis was not limited to primary care clinics. KHC insured most hospitalized patients, both in its own hospitals (e.g., Beilinson, Kaplan, Carmel and Soroka) and in state-owned hospitals. KHC's financial constraints meant that it was not able to pay state hospitals for their services. Thus, large state-owned hospitals such as Tel Hashomer, Barzilai, and Poria struggled as well. At the primary care clinics, expensive drugs such as Losec or Ocsaar were scarce, doctors had difficulty referring patients to the hospital's specialist services, and this, in turn, led to long lines for specialist services and elective surgeries.

Ms. Malka's story, relayed in the Introduction, was one of the many expressions of this crisis. As a chronically ill patient with low income, she had no option but to remain with KHC and suffer the consequences of the crisis. Neither the Maccabi nor the Meuhedet sick funds would accept her as a patient because of her chronic condition, and she could not afford to receive care or buy drugs in the private sector. The case of another patient, Sivan Or, was similar. Suffering from recurrent bouts of retinal detachment, she was also deeply dissatisfied with KHC. She had been treated at a hospital in Jerusalem, where she used to live. But when she moved to Jaffa, KHC denied her request to continue her follow up at the Hadassah hospital in Jerusalem because costs in Hadassah were higher than in the hospitals in the Tel Aviv-Jaffa area. She wanted to leave to become a member of the Maccabi sick fund, but they did not accept her because she suffered from a chronic condition.

For myself and many of my colleagues, this was a particularly difficult time. As a medical student in Argentina I had known many, many patients who could not afford medicines for treatable conditions. As part of my medical education I had worked at the emergency room of a public hospital in San Miguel, one of Buenos Aires' poor suburbs. I quickly understood that patients kept coming back to the ER because they were not able to afford the medications they needed. We had several patients suffering from congestive heart failure who came every few days with pulmonary edema, not so much because of the severity of their condition but because they were not able to buy their medications. We also saw children who suffered from asthmatic attacks who came to the hospital for inhalation treatment with a bronchodilator such as Ventolin because they had no money to have one at home. I remember once going with an ambulance to assist a very sick asthmatic child who lived in a one-room house, slept on the floor, and received no treatment (what a sad irony that the name of his street was Bela Bartok!—such a sophisticated name for such poverty).

We often discharged people from the emergency room with recommendations for treatment knowing that those were only virtual recommendations. Later, as a hospital resident in Israel, I learned to appreciate the difference between a public health service that guarantees an acceptable standard of care and a public health care system that provides only a safety net for those with no access to the private system. When I first came to Israel, I worked at the Barzilai hospital in Ashkelon, a city in the southern periphery of Israel with significant poverty. As everywhere, the relationship between poverty (or low socioeconomic status) and disease was evident. Even though a high percentage of the hospital's patients were poor, however, most were members of one of the public sick funds and had access to a relatively broad spectrum of services and drugs. When we discharged someone home from the emergency room or after hospitalization, I knew that he or she had access to follow-up by a primary care physician and would get most medications (for sure for basic drugs such as bronchodilators and first-line treatment for congestive heart failure). With my Argentinean experience still fresh, I appreciated the difference in Israel. Yet, here I was, some ten years later, presiding over a clinic as patients saw their access to certain services limited because they did not have the money to afford to purchase them privately. Malka and my other patients were victims of this transformation. Her story and that of Sivan symbolized the beginning of a change.

As the neoliberalization of the health care service in Israel deepened, private expenditure increased faster than total health expenditure. National health expenditure, at fixed prices, rose 43 percent between 1986 and 1994. During the same years, spending in dentistry grew 62 percent and private expenditure (drugs, physicians, and equipment) 59 percent. During the 1979/80 to 1989/90 period, growth in expenditure for private services rose by 52 percent. From 1990 to 1994, private expenditure rose another 17 percent (CBS 2003). The most rapid increase in expenditure was for private doctors (excluding dental care), an expenditure that rose 102 percent in the 1980s and another 32 percent until 1994 (Chernichovsky 1991; CBS 2003).

In the 1980s, the average annual growth rate in private health expenditure was more than 86.3 percent, compared with an approximately 2.7 percent increase in national health expenditure during the same period (Chernichovsky 1991). The shift of funding from government to households, the shift of the financially better-off from KHC to the smaller sick funds, and the expansion of private insurance schemes all increased inequality in access to health care.[5]

Since health care insurance was not mandatory, some 7 percent of the population in Israel (mostly among the poor) was uninsured. There were real differences in the quality of health care that the richer sick funds provided when compared with KHC. Health care in the periphery was of lower quality, both because KHC was the sole provider in the geographic periphery and because the number and quality of health care facilities was much greater in the big cities. Hospitals in the Tel Aviv, Jerusalem, and Haifa areas were considered better than those in periphery cities such as Naharyia, Ashkelon, or Zefat. The number of specialists per capita was (and remains) much higher in the big cities, and more sophisticated technology such as computerized tomography (CT) also remains more accessible there than in the periphery. Last but not least, there were significant differences between the quality of services received by Jewish and Palestinian citizens. The latter received poorer health care because of the high percentage of uninsured (24%) among them and because most Palestinians lived in the periphery and were insured by KHC.

There was such a strong public feeling that the health care system was in crisis that the government nominated a state commission with the mandate to investigate the reasons for the crisis and propose solutions.[6] The National Health Insurance law passed in 1994 was one of the main results of the crisis and of the commission's suggestions.

The Legislation of National Health Insurance

Geographic, ethnic, and citizenship status had influenced access to health care services since the founding of the state of Israel in 1948. The privatization process described above, however, created a multitiered health care system in which income became a more important factor in the kind of services you received. As is often the case, in capitalistic societies, when it came to the lack of services, the last (the people of lower socioeconomic status) came first—with Palestinians in the Occupied Territories and foreign workers having no health insurance. The next tier included Israeli citizens without health insurance. Some 7 percent of the Israeli population lacked health insurance. Israeli Arabs were overrepresented among this group, with 24 percent of them without health insurance. The uninsured had free access to public hospitals and to preventive medicine. However, they did not have free access to primary or ambulatory care, and they had to pay full price for medications. The third level of the multitiered system included the members of KHC, where per-capita spending was NIS 2,533—a sum that had to cover an older, poorer, and sicker population (requiring more, not less, expenditure per capita). The next level was that of the smaller sick funds—Maccabi, Meuhedet, and Leumit—where per-capita spending was NIS 2,970 for a younger and healthier population. Finally, the pinnacle were the very rich, who could afford to buy private—fee-for-service—health care.

As we have already seen, the financial strain on KHC, combined with its age composition and case-mix (as well as its bureaucratic organization), led its younger, healthier, and better-off members to the small sick funds. I remember when a young woman came to my office to ask why her father did not receive a referral to the hospital he wanted. He had been a member of KHC all his life, she told me. It was inconceivable that now that he was 74 years old, he could not go to the hospital he wanted. I tried to explain that KHC had preferred hospitals to which patients were referred. She indignantly retorted that at Maccabi, her sick fund, something like that would never happen.

She then informed me that she did not pay Maccabi more than she had previously paid at KHC, but she had access to the best specialists and was never told that a drug was not available. "When I come to ask something for my father I am so glad I moved to Maccabi!" I asked her politely why she didn't convince her father to become a member of Maccabi.

She replied matter-of-factly, "Well, I would have taken him with me to Maccabi when my husband and I left KHC, but they would not accept him because of his age. They do not accept old people." Interestingly, she did not seem to realize the link between Maccabi's rejection of old people like her father and the fact that she was able to receive services that were not available to her father at KHC. It was as though she and her father lived in parallel health care universes connected only by her complaints but not by any deeper understanding of the realities of health care financing. It did not occur to her that the Maccabi sick fund could afford to give her Cadillac services because of the money it saved by not covering high-risk, high-cost members like her father.

This young woman was full of complaints about the public system she had abandoned (and to which she had abandoned her father) and praise for Maccabi, the one she'd entered to which her father could not be accepted. Her attitude is a quite widespread phenomenon in contemporary Israel and expresses the dramatic weakening of solidarity that had hitherto linked both the middle- and lower classes and the young and old.[7] Her attitudes mirror the ways in which Israeli society has Americanized over the past two and a half decades. As we saw in chapter 1, until the beginning of the 1980s, Israelis thought of themselves in the first-person plural not singular. They viewed themselves as part of a group rather than as individuals making choices for themselves alone, so much so that their choice of physician was determined by their political party and community. Now, Israelis (particularly younger Israelis), like the Americans who have had such a strong impact on Israeli society and identity, view themselves as discrete individuals whose choices affect only themselves. Or as Segev writes, "Americanization has weakened social solidarity and, in contrast with original Israeli Zionism, has made the individual the center point of life" (Segev 1991). The term *American* as a comment on a service or a product is used in Israel to express admiration. The phenomenon is particularly paradoxical when it concerns the health care system. The U.S. health care system, with its more than $7,000 per capita expenditure, its 47 million uninsured, and its poor outcomes, can hardly count as an example of excellence (Kuminsky 2008). The process of Americanization is a global one, but in Israel it has been more deep and radical because of the geopolitical and military dependence on the United States.

Until the beginning of the 1980s, this powerful sense of group identity was reflected in the fact that there was no difference in the age-mix of the various sick funds. Between 1981 and 1994, the percentage of members older than sixty-five in KHC rose from 9.4 percent to 13 percent, while in Leumit it fell from 8.7 percent to 7.2 percent, in Maccabi from 6.1 percent to 4.8 percent, and in Meuhedet from 8.3 percent to 4.1 percent (Rosen et al. 1995). KHC also had a higher percentage of chronically ill members (even within a given age group). "Cream-skimming"—the selection of younger and healthier (and hence potentially cheaper) members—and "negative selection"—the rejection of potentially expensive members—deepened the differences among the sick funds.[8]

This was done very simply. Maccabi and Meuhedet did not accept patients older than sixty-five and also rejected patients suffering from chronic conditions, even relatively simple ones (e.g., somebody with a previous detachment of the retina). Between 1981 and 1994, the membership of the smaller sick funds increased from 8 percent to 37 percent of the insured population, while membership in KHC decreased from 82.3 percent in 1981 to 62.1 percent in 1995 (Bin Nun and Greenblat, 1999). As I said earlier, many young people left KHC during this time, mostly to the Maccabi sick fund but also to Meuhedet, while their older parents remained in KHC because the smaller sick funds would not accept them. As with the young woman angry that her father was not referred to the hospital he wanted, most of those young people did not seem to be aware that their abandonment of KHC meant that the quality of care their parents would receive would be worse. They did not seem to realize that the taxes they paid in the past supported the health care needs of the elderly since the younger use much less care. The average cost for a patient between the ages of twenty to thirty-five is less than ten times the cost for a patient older than seventy-five. The simple facts of health care financing show the close relation between cream-skimming at one sick fund and poor services at the other. Young people who left KHC for Maccabi complained about the poor services their parents received at the former, without realizing that by their leaving KHC they severed the links of solidarity between young and old, and that was one of the main reasons for this state of things.

The transition to this neoliberal model resulted in a crisis caused by the underfunding of the system and the severe financial strain on KHC—still the biggest HMO. This spilled over to public hospitals, which, in turn, produced growing public dissatisfaction with the system as a whole. This dissatisfaction was everywhere. I encountered it at the clinic, each time one of our patients did not find the drug one of our doctors prescribed at the pharmacy. I met it when children I referred to elective surgery had to wait for more than six months for a tonsillectomy. I heard it from friends working at hospitals, who complained about the difficulties in buying new equipment. When the Israeli Medical Association publicly demanded a deep reform of the health care system, this was a clear expression of this broader discontent. This dissatisfaction was also expressed in both the Knesset and the media, where there was increasing pressure for a reform of the public health care system.

The crisis was resolved, at least temporarily, by the legislation of the NHI law. The legislation of the NHI law is remarkable because it went against the neoliberalizing trend that affected all welfare services. Several factors combined in a unique way to allow the passage of the law. The pervasive perception that the system was in crisis; the influence of the main researchers in the field of health policy and health economy; the backing of the right-wing Likud party that saw in the law a way of weakening the Histadrut; the political interest of the Labor party's young leaders, who also wanted to weaken the Histadrut establishment: All these processes came together in the passing of the NHI law.

The new law recognized health care as a right, underlined the importance of equality in access to health care, and guaranteed a universal health "basket" to every Israeli resident. In so doing, the law expanded the insured population by the inclusion of the 4–7 percent of the population who were not insured by any of the sick funds until 1994. Most of the uninsured were Israeli Palestinians or people with low incomes.

In its first article the law decreed that national health insurance in Israel would be based on "principles of justice, equality, and mutual help" (NHI law 1994). Every inhabitant had the right to health care services, and the state was responsible for the funding of the health care "basket of services." This basket adopted an enlarged version of the basket of services provided by KHC. It included full hospitalization coverage without any time limit, full primary care services, and a generous spectrum of diagnostic procedures and medications. The system was to be financed by an earmarked "health tax" (4.8% of income), by the (already existent) earmarked employer tax, and by the government (from the general budget). The National Insurance Institute (NII) would collect the first two taxes.

The NHI law determined that the monies collected by the NII would be distributed among the sick funds according to a formula that would take into account the number of members in each sick fund and their age-mix. If the funds collected by the NII fell below "the cost of the basket of services" as determined by the ministers of health and finance, then the gap would be covered by general revenues. This was a key statement because, with it, the government took full responsibility for the financing of the health care services included in the "health basket."

The NHI law seemed to suggest that, in the field of health care at least, the state was adopting a different approach than the private, market-based approach to the welfare system as a whole. By acknowledging health care as a right, stressing equality of access and stating government responsibility, the law was a step toward a more public and equal health care service. It made health insurance mandatory and guaranteed access to health care even to those not paying the health tax, thus cutting the link between ability to pay and entitlement to health care. The universalization of insurance entitled between 250,000 and 300,000 uninsured people to health care. Since the enforcement of the law in 1995, there has been greater competition among the sick funds over members from peripheral regions, low-income areas, and Arab cities. Since the monies that the sick funds receive are not dependent on the members' income and the Arab population is relatively young, Israeli Arabs began to represent an attractive sector for the sick funds. Such competition has resulted in better facilities and improved service levels in previously neglected areas.

This change in the sick funds' approach to the health care needs of the Israeli Palestinians was reflected in reports that found that Israeli Palestinians were more satisfied with the health care system. Research done in 1995, a year after the legislation of the NHI law, showed that 70 percent of the Israeli Palestinians considered that the health care system had improved since the implementation of the NHI law. However, this improvement was the result of a change in the way the sick funds were financed and their interest in appealing to the Arab population and not the result of a planned policy whose goal was to close age-old gaps in health care accessibility and health status between the Jewish and the Arab citizens.

The NHI law, nevertheless, made the system more equal, and in redistributing funds among the four sick funds, it narrowed the gap between them. The difference between the four sick funds' per capita spending became smaller, ranging from NIS 2658 to NIS 2722 in 1995 (less than 3% difference). The law also put an end to open "cream-skimming" by the smaller funds, stating that every sick fund had to accept every citizen applying for membership. The system became less multitiered, as the gap between the sick funds narrowed. Revenues as stipulated by the NHI law increased, in per capita terms, by 11 percent at Clalit and 7 percent at Leumit, while declining by 15 percent at Maccabi and 7 percent at Meuhedet. Between 1994 and 1996 age-adjusted per capita operating expenditure dropped in three of the four sick funds. It declined by almost 9 percent in Leumit, over 8 percent in Maccabi, and almost 5 percent in Meuhedet, while in Clalit there was an increase of almost 5 percent.

Even though the NHI legislation restrained the privatization process, it did not bring the public/private rate in the financing of health expenditures back to the levels of the late 1970s. In 1995, household out-of-pocket spending still represented 25 percent of the national health expenditure (CBS 2000). Moreover, even though it compensated sick funds for the different age-mix of their members, the law did not affect the disparity generated by differences in case-mix and income mix (two variables related to health care services utilization).[9] Finally, the adjustment of the health basket cost does not take into account demographics (i.e., the growth of the population as a result of births, immigration, and population aging), and it allows for a very limited inclusion of technological innovations. Thus, in the future, it is possible that the public health basket will be unable to provide all the care and services people need, which will then lead to the reconstitution of a multitiered health care system. Such problems notwithstanding, the NHI law—the major health care reform of the last two decades—partially bucked the privatization trend.

Neoliberalism Advances, 1997–2005

The legislation of the NHI law represented only a temporary solution to the health care system's crisis. In 1997, only two years after the application of the NHI law, the government eliminated the employers' contribution to health care. This generated a significant loss of resources that was supposed to be covered by government payments from general revenues. While the employers' tax was paid by a sector of the population that enjoys a greater income and a better economic position, general revenues are paid by the population as a whole. Eliminating this source of funding not only deprived the health care system of an earmarked tax but also diminished the redistributive effect that the employers' tax had.

The main attack on a more equal public health care system took place one year after. In 1998, the Treasury proposed a "Budget Reconciliation bill" that included the following key features:

1. Each sick fund would determine the specific health services it would offer as well as its member fees without a universal law to set standards.
2. Copayments with means testing and a monthly fee (income-independent) tax, a "head tax" would substitute for government financing.
3. The government would not automatically bridge the gap between the cost of the health basket and the funds distributed by the NII since the supplement to the basket of services from the national budget would be a nominal sum.
4. For-profit sick funds would be allowed to enter the health care market.
5. Copayment for medicines would significantly increase.

The proposed reforms represented a blow to the decoupling of individual income and access to health care. It also represented a partial retreat from the government's responsibility for the provision of health care services. Popular opposition blocked some of the measures included in the original proposal (such as the "head tax," the approval of a for-profit sick fund, and the sick funds' right to curtail services included in the health basket). However, even after the changes, the bill seriously impaired the achievements of the NHI law.[10]

The 1998 bill challenged (at least de facto) the state's responsibility for the provision of a common "health basket" to every citizen. The Budget Reconciliation bill set a fixed state expenditure for health care, thus freeing the state from its obligation to cover the gap between the health tax revenue and the actual cost of the health basket. Under the new law, such an obligation fell to the sick funds. In order to fulfill it, the sick funds would have to become more efficient—that is, cut costs and transfer some of the costs to patients. The share of the sick funds costs financed directly by users (as copayments) grew considerably after 1997. In 1997 copayments represented 5.6 percent of the sick funds' total budget, and in 2004 it reached 14.4 percent.

The 1997 and 1998 Budget Reconciliation laws opened the way for the ongoing shift of financing from the state to individual households. As a consequence the government's share of the national health expenditure is declining every year, shifting costs to the public in the form of out-of pocket paying or private insurance. In 1995, when the NHI law was first implemented, the government financed 75 percent of the national expenditure in health, and private expenditure covered the other 25 percent. In 1999, the government's share went down to 69.4 percent, and private funding climbed to 29 percent. For the next decade, the government's share declined further, to 65.2 percent in 2005, when private financing reached 30.7 percent of the national health expenditure.

The shift of health care financing from the public to the private represents a more regressive and unequal way of financing health care services and has negative consequences on access to health care. For example, in a survey by the Israeli Medical Association 25 percent of households reported that they had not bought medications due to their high cost. These were mostly elderly people with low incomes or Israeli Palestinians. Members of each of these groups reported that they could not buy all the drugs prescribed by their doctors. Sadly, twenty years after I arrived in Israel from Argentina, the Israeli poor also had to give up buying some of the medication that they need. A system that, for the poor at least, had taken many giant steps forward was now taking significant steps backward.

The statistical map of household expenditure reflected all these changes and more. In 2001, health care represented 3.8 percent of total household expenditure; in 2004, it represented 4.9% of total household expenditure. While total household expenditure grew 24 percent between 1997 and 2001, the households' expenditure in health grew 60 percent (Chernichowski et al. 2003). The most affluent 20 percent of the population spent almost three times as much as the poorest 20 percent in 1997 and almost four times as much in 2004. The trend continues to the present. The poorest and sickest people now bear much heavier burdens than the wealthy and had less access to services. They cannot buy all the medications their doctors prescribe, cannot afford complementary insurance that allows access to newer cancer treatment, and have almost no access to dental services.

Privatization of Ownership

Private ownership of health care facilities is the next way the system has moved from a public service toward a more profit-dominated enterprise that opens new areas for capital accumulation. In Israel, private health care participation in national health expenditure rose from 18.9 percent in 1984 to 23.3 percent in 1993 (CBS 2001). The number of private hospitals went up from 57 in 1980 to 94 in 1993, even though their share did not change, since the number of public hospitals also increased. Yet the private sector's share of general hospital beds *did* rise, from 2.9 percent to 3.6 percent between 1980 and 1989, and in 1993 it reached 4 percent of the total; private geriatric beds grew from 29 percent to 34 percent in the same period (Bin Nun and Chinitz 1993), reaching 37 percent in 1993. The number of hospital beds illustrates the rate of growth in the private sector: while the number of hospital beds in the public sector grew 14.4 percent in the 1980–1993 period, the number of beds in the private sector grew 50 percent.[11] In areas such as nursing care, privatization has been the preferred trend, and plans for construction of new units were—and still are—focused mostly on the private sector. Indeed, part of the development of the private sector is financed by public funds: Almost a third of the services sold by the private sector are bought by the four public sick funds.

In 1985 the business sector represented almost 19 percent of the national health expenditure, and in 1993, the year before the legislation of NHI, the business sector's share had increased to 24 percent. In the same period the government's share decreased from 24 percent to 20 percent, while the nonprofit and sick funds' shares remained unchanged.

Health services also became a growing and profitable business. In the mid-1980s the private sector provided almost 19 percent of the total expenditure in health, which was then NIS 800 million. Eight years later, in 1993, it increased to 23.3 percent, and the total expenditure had grown to NIS 2,864 million. In other words, the private health care sector had grown from a 152 million business to an almost 700 million one.

The growth of the private sector not only includes direct provision of services but also the growth of the private insurance market.[12] Traditionally, there was only one Israeli company—Shiloah—that sold health care insurance policies. The expansion of the private health insurance market led insurance companies that previously did not specialize in health care to develop health insurance programs. Private insurers in Israel, as in the United States, can choose the kinds of people, disorders, and procedures they want to cover, and their goal is to pay as little in services as they can by attracting the younger, healthier, and wealthier (Light 1997).

In the Israeli system, the public sector actually subsidized the increase in private ownership and private profits. The Nursing Care Law—which allows private entrepreneurs to provide care that is financed from public sources—is an example of how public funds are used to subsidize private profits. In 1988, before the enforcement of this law, there were only thirteen organizations (some of them nonprofit and some of them for-profit) providing home nursing services, in 1991 there were eighty-four, and all the new ones were for-profit (Gal 1994).

The privatization process is not limited to the financing of expenditures, but—as it did during the pre-NHI law period—also comprises the provision of services. In the first years after the legislation of the NHI law, private-sector services represented 23 percent of the national health expenditure. Following the 1998 Budget Reconciliation law, there was a sustained increase in the private sector share, which reached 26 percent in 1999. The private sector increased even more during the 2000s, and in 2003 its share of the health sector was 27 percent.[13]

The 2005 and 2006 budget dramatically encouraged privatization trends—producing the complete privatization of complex geriatric care and the privatization of laboratory services for geriatric and psychiatric hospitals. The government also changed the institutional character of two of the biggest state-owned hospitals—Tel Hashomer and Rambam. From now on they will be managed by an autonomous board of directors, will be responsible for their budget (and not entitled to government coverage of possible deficits), will directly employ their workers, and will function as a business for all purposes.

Turning Health Care into a Business

In 1998, KHC's new management set out to train managers of their primary care clinics. As part of their training program, they published a booklet, titled "TTT: Train the Trainer," to introduce us (I was one of the directors of a clinic) to the world of *new public management* (NPM)—the theory that provides the rationale bringing market-based approaches into national, publicly funded health care systems across the globe. New public management emphasizes cost-containment and prods administrators to focus on operational efficiency.

The booklet I received from the directors of KHC was a tutorial in the new ethos of the Israeli health care system. What it tried to teach physicians and other caregivers was how to shed their service orientation and adopt a businesslike approach to patient care—whether they worked at the front desk as receptionists greeting patients, as doctors diagnosing and treating, or as accountants or administrators.

Both the public sick funds and the public hospitals have been encouraged to transform their institutional culture and work organization according to models developed in the for-profit business sector. In response, public hospitals and the public sick funds began to offer private services such as imaging or diagnostic institutes or centers for plastic surgery. "Patients" or "members" morphed into "clients" or "consumers." Services began to be "outsourced," and permanent workers replaced by temporary employees. Recalcitrant doctors, nurses, and administrators are pressed to think in business terms because hospitals and sick funds—not the state—now have the major financial responsibility for institutional survival. Advocates of privatization insist that the transformation of the "patient" into a "customer," and the doctor or hospital into a "provider," is justified because the market is always the most efficient vehicle to distribute resources, and the private sector is, by definition, more efficient than the public one. What NPM advocates want is not a system driven by health care needs and an ethics of care but by economic "efficiency" and the ethics of the market. In their idealization of market economy, they are blind to the fact that submitting the field of health care to the designs of the market is problematic not only from the point of view of public health and medical ethics but also in terms of efficiency, as anyone familiar with health care in the United States can attest.

KHC, modeled after the German and Austrian workers' sick funds, began a process of organizational change dominated by the push to adopt the private sector's organizational culture. It now faced increased competition as well as the fact that a significant percentage of its most affluent and young members left for the Maccabi and Meuhedet sick funds in the late 1980s and early 1990s. KHC physicians were told they had no other choice but to change or wither. The change in the state's approach to the financing of health care, cuts in subsidies, and the consequent financial crisis compelled the new managers at KHC to adopt a managerial philosophy imported from the business world. This philosophy was extended to the organization as a whole through the combination of training and education, co-optation, and managerial pressure on employees.

Turning KHC into a business involved the decentralization of responsibility and the centralization of strategic command. The decentralization process transformed each of KHC's eight geographic districts into a separate economic unit, responsible for the services it should provide, its budget, and the marketing of those services. The goal of each unit was to provide services within the limits of a budget distributed by the central management. Not only did each unit have to live within its budget, but it had to make sure its clients (i.e., former patients) registered satisfaction with the "product lines" we were now delivering.

Decentralization does not, however, end at the level of the district, but runs all the way up to the level of the primary care clinic. Each clinic is being transformed into an economic unit in charge of its own budget[14] and receives a budget calculated according to the number of people it serves and the history of its previous costs. The clinic must provide the services guaranteed by the NHI law while still remaining within this budget. In addition, every year each unit must produce a working plan to comply with cost control, client satisfaction, and quality of care goals. Every unit must also reach out to members who might move to another sick fund, design ways to diminish hospitalization or reduce the number of referrals to hospital outpatient clinics, and refer patients to the sick fund's own specialist clinics. Front-line units are responsible not only for cost control but also for marketing their activities to recruit new clients, improving the age- and case-mix composition of KHC's membership, achieving client satisfaction, and improving quality of service. Physicians were recruited as managers of the front-line units. Although the process includes a degree of empowerment of front-line units, which are less dependent on central authorities, the main goal of the process undoubtedly is cost-containment, and strategic command remains centralized.

As I said above, to engage us in the new managerial culture, I and fellow physicians received a booklet called "Train the Trainer," which explained our task as directors within the new organizational philosophy. When we leafed through the pages of the booklet we learned that we, physicians trained to diagnose and treat the sick, were suddenly supposed to be "medical managers" who were responsible for all health care activities regarding the insured population belonging to the clinics we managed.

We were told that we must take on this responsibility and shift our thinking accordingly if our clinics were to comply with budget limitations while simultaneously providing good-quality health care and improving the members' case-mix.

In typical U.S. management-speak, the booklet informed us that every medical manager must start by "working on him/herself" and by "assessing his/her own position on the process and its goals" in order to become an "agent of change" (Yahav-KHC 1997). As agents of change, we stood at the top of a hierarchy in which we were held responsible not only for our own practice but for the actions and business acumen of our subordinates, while also being accountable to our superiors. To achieve the institutional goals (which we would now consider our own goals), we must lead and patrol the activities and attitudes of other physicians, nurses, and administrative and ancillary workers. As medical directors and individual physicians we were also responsible for their patient's expenditures. As physicians have been told to do in U.S. managed care organizations, when making clinical decisions, each of us should, from now on, also take into account the cost-effectiveness of the different treatments she/he provides.

Surveillance and control at KHC (and also at the other sick funds) are achieved through a variety of mechanisms. Administrators at the district's central management office gather data through utilization reviews, consumer satisfaction polls, and quality-of-service and quality-of-care indicators, and they feed this back to each individual physician. Every three months I received a folder with data that included reports on the cost of each physician's prescriptions, the hospitalization costs of each of our patients, which drugs we prescribed, and whether any of us prescribed too many "second choice" drugs (i.e., drugs that, because of cost, should be reserved only for cases in which first-line drugs would not work).

Administrators also established "quality groups" where the workers must supervise and control their own behavior and attitudes; and individual evaluation meetings with the clinic's personnel. The quality groups discussed the aspects of everyday tasks in order to find ways to become more efficient (i.e., reduce costs) and improve the quality of service. The goal of individual meetings was to give each worker positive or negative feedback on his or her work. As the director of a clinic, I was expected to have periodic meetings with each of the workers (administrative personnel, nurses, physicians, pharmacists) to discuss what they were doing well and the areas in which they should improve their performance. These meetings did not focus on clinical practice but rather on issues related to consumer satisfaction and cost-containment.

Through computerized data (purchase of services, lab utilization, prescriptions), medical managers—and the district authorities—scrutinized the performance of every physician (both by measuring indicators of quality of care and the expenses s/he incurs) and the cost of every patient. The computerization of the patient's medical history transforms the organization into a Panoptikon of sorts, where each level can see the lower level's performance without being seen. The central management surveys each medical director's performance, while the latter may follow each physician's performance.

As I said, once every three months I received data concerning our performance as a clinic. The data included the expenditures of each physician's patients and how they stood when compared with the whole district. The data included hospitalization costs, costs of referral to specialists at the hospitals' outpatient clinics and to specialists at KHC's facilities, the cost of laboratory tests, and the cost of drugs. For me as a director, and for each of the physicians, this data was supposed to make us aware of costs and encourage efforts to limit expenditures. There was no open or veiled threat. The central management assumed that if we were more aware of the structure of expenditures we would be able to manage ourselves. The district administrators did recommend that each clinic should try to limit referrals to hospitals' outpatient clinics and instead utilize KHC's own specialists. There were also preferred drugs, since generics are less expensive than brand drugs. Of course, I believe that it is legitimate for a public, nonprofit sick fund to try to rationalize and limit costs. We are not speaking about a for-profit HMO that cuts costs at the expense of patients' needs in order to increase shareholders' dividends. In the public system, saving on unnecessary expenditures (e.g., shifting from brand names to generics) means more resources for the population as a whole. The public health care system has not only the right, but in a way the duty, to rationalize costs insofar as it does not influence the quality of care. The use of brand names or "me-too drugs" does not contribute to better standards of care, only to the profits of the pharmaceutical companies. The problem was that the organizational change was not limited to an attempt to rationalize costs but implied the adoption of a business model that considers health care as one more commodity to be bought and sold in the marketplace.

Even patient satisfaction was defined in business terms—as if our "clients" were visiting a department store or staying overnight in a hotel. For example, we received quarterly satisfaction surveys, which showed us the degree of patients' satisfaction (or dissatisfaction) with the various services we provided at the clinic: doctors, nurses, administrative services, pharmacy. We were expected to discuss ways to improve the degree of patients' satisfaction: diminishing waiting times, "improving" the way we answered the phone, suggesting initiatives to make our "customers" happier. Even though there were no "disciplinary measures" taken against physicians or nurses who did not comply with this new organizational model, the customer-oriented model modified the way we saw ourselves within the institution. The new organizational model created also a burdensome feeling among health care providers because the administration, in its own words, wanted "more for less" from us. Thus, while none of us disagreed with the goal of increasing patient satisfaction, decreasing wait times, or making our clients happier, we all wondered how we were to do this when we had higher patient loads, less time to see patients, fewer staff to answer phone calls, and less time to come up with the "initiatives" that would make our "clients" more satisfied.

The change in the physician's role was and is not limited to his/her curbing costs. Within the new business culture, the medical encounter becomes not only an input, central in determining costs, but also an output, a commodity that is marketed and evaluated in businesslike terms. The physician becomes part of the sick fund's marketing strategy. In the late 1990s, KHC, for example, conducted a market study. The report concluded that dissatisfaction with the doctor-patient relationship was an important factor in a user's decision to abandon the sick fund. To address the problem, KHC commissioned a qualitative study that tried to determine which characteristics of the encounter make it satisfactory or unsatisfactory for "clients." With this knowledge, the KHC management invited physicians, patients, health educators, human resources managers, and marketing specialists to take part in a "think tank" of sorts to discuss the characteristics of the medical encounter in terms of enhancing consumer satisfaction.

I was one of the physicians invited to participate in the brainstorming process. It consisted of four meetings in which we were informed about the results of the survey and about the need to think about ways to improve the doctor-patient relationship. Administrators warned us that we were losing a lot of members to the other sick funds: When asked why they left KHC, a significant number of patients answered that they were not satisfied with the way doctors treated them. We were asked to consider the roots of the bad doctor-patient relationship and to figure out ways to improve the way doctors treated their clients. I, for one, would have been happy to have better relationships with my patients in the sense of having a relationship that would enhance their health and empower them. Management, however, was not motivated by any interest in enhancing the therapeutic value of a good bond between doctor and patient but wanted us to engage in a competitive bidding war to keep "clients" from leaving our sick fund and moving to another. Physicians, nurses, and other professionals were not asked to engage in a reflection—which would have been appropriate and perhaps even long overdue—about what might improve patient health and well-being. We were asked to beat the competition.

The reluctance of physicians like myself to participate in this process of caregiver reeducation and a redefinition of the clinical encounter hardly made a dent in the attempt to transform sick funds like KHC. Administrators continued to pursue their business strategy by issuing "guidelines" for a satisfactory (from the consumer's point of view) medical encounter and to present these guidelines to "focus groups." These focus groups consisted of KHC members who had said they had been thinking about leaving KHC for another sick fund. They were presented with the guidelines, the coordinators registered their reactions, and the final guidelines were adapted to these reactions. The meetings in which I took part were the beginning of a long process that ended in a series of workshops for primary care physicians to train us to improve the way we treated our "clients." The workshops were supposed to help us improve our communication skills, teaching us how to relate to the "client," how to cope with angry "customers," and how to explain to our "clients" in a polite way that there were certain drugs that were not included in the health basket or that we could refer them only to preferred hospitals and not to any hospital they chose. In essence, we were being told we must please the customer while simultaneously telling the customer—in a kinder and gentler manner—that he or she could never get the services where, when, or how they wanted them. What we were being asked to do was not to transform the content of our relationships with patients but to transform its façade.

Approaching the medical encounter as a marketing problem exemplifies the way in which what used to be a very personal relationship was now viewed and transformed into a commodity to be sold in a newly created health care marketplace.[15]

The significant implications of this transformation can be understood when one looks at what it means to turn a "patient" into a "client" and an encounter that is supposed to be guided by an ethical commitment into one guided by the ethics of the market. Although some of us don't live up to this high moral standard, physicians like myself take the Hippocratic oath to "first, do no harm." That is, at least, the ethical ideal of health care as service. It is an ideal that places responsibility to "do no harm" on the physician, nurse, or other clinician rather than on the patient. When one turns a "patient" into a "client," or even worse, a "customer," the ethical balance shifts dramatically. The ethic of the marketplace is expressed succinctly in the motto, *caveat emptor* ("buyer beware"). In other words, it is up to the customer to protect him- or herself, not to the doctor or organization to protect the patient.

As we have seen, the "enterprising" process includes such changes in language not only at the level of the clinic but also at the level of the organization. In recent years, the sick fund changed its name from Kupat Holim Clalit (General Sick Fund) to Clalit Sherutei Briut (General Health Services, or CHS)[16] to both sever its link with the old worker's fund and emphasize its "service-oriented" character. Members—who were once called *chaverim* (Hebrew for "members" or "comrades")—became "clients" or "consumers." (in Hebrew, "lekuhot") Yitzhak Peterburg, CHS' CEO between 1997 and 2002, stated the transformation when he claimed: "In the last few years CHS has undergone a service and strategic revolution...[I]t has been transformed from a sick fund into a health organization providing a broad range of services, and considers its goal to be: Encouraging its clients to lead a healthy life" (Peterburg 2001, 38). CHS is now "focused on the client." Peterburg makes clear that "[t]he conception centered on the client [client and not patient or member] expresses itself in the organization's vision of the client as its most important resource" (ibid).

In an interview at the time of his resignation as CHS CEO in 2002, Peterburg announced that: "During the last five years CHS has realized many important goals...It went through a strategic marketing revolution, it strengthened its financial basis...We may conclude that CHS has evolved into a business organization in every respect" (CHS 2002).

One of the most noteworthy consequences of this "evolution" into a "business organization" was the exacerbation of ageism in what was once a far less discriminatory—at least for Israeli Jews—system. Despite Peterburg's claim, the focus was not on *every* "client." The focus was on "clients" who were attractive because they cost less. Because the elderly are sicker and use more services, one of the organization's goals was to "improve" the "age mix" of the membership, as Peterburg euphemistically put it in a meeting with directors of KHC clinics in the Tel Aviv district at which I was a participant.

As we sat in a conference room, Peterburg showed us charts with the age-related profile of our members compared with those of the other sick funds. There on the minute charting of KHC members, we could see that our patients suffered from an incurable and thus fatal disease—they were older than members of other sick funds. They thus consumed far more— and far more costly—health care services. Peterburg warned us that the current age-mix endangered KHC's future because in a decade or two the number of members between ages of twenty and forty would not sustain as big an organization as KHC. When I directly asked him whether he was telling us to deliberately attract younger "clients," he replied candidly that if we cared about our jobs, that is exactly what we should do.

The operational consequence of this was that KHC invested more in developing services aimed at the young. District administrators who took Peterburg's words to heart initiated local initiatives that blatantly discriminated against older and sicker KHC members. One of those initiatives, for example, was to reduce the waiting times for specialist services for members who were thirty-five and younger. Every specialist was informed that he or she should leave free slots in their schedule so that younger members would not have to wait more than twenty-four hours for an appointment. Older members were allocated to the regular queue, and had to wait two to three weeks for an appointment. At one of the clinics, nurses' services were organized so that younger members would not have to wait for blood tests. The clinic referred to this as VIP service.

Physicians and nurses usually do not openly oppose such initiatives. This was too much for some of them, however, who informed journalists about these "initiatives," forcing the KHC Tel Aviv district to stop them. Deliberate strategies were thus developed to service "consumers" who would consume less, and physicians were encouraged or coerced into incorporating the requirements of this businesslike approach to their clinical or patient care agenda.

As a result of the government's decision in the late 1990s to transform public hospitals into "closed economic institutions," the government was no longer responsible for the hospitals' deficits. The latter must balance their budgets so that expenditure meets income (Shirom and Amit 1996, 50). The declared goals of the new government policy were to curb costs, promote efficiency, and enhance competence (Shalom and Harison 1996). Public hospitals increased profitable activities, such as coronary bypasses and cardiac catheterization, and rewarded physicians who increased those activities.[17]

Public hospitals began to compete for patients. They developed new services, such as routine physical examinations that they provided for managers of large companies and advertised to the public (Chinitz and Rosen 1991). As estimated by Gabi Bin Nun (then the deputy general director of the MOH), by the late 1990s, 90 percent of hospitals activities were related to the health basket and 10 percent were activities sold by hospitals (Bin Nun 1999). More than 70 percent of public hospitals were allowed to sell private services up to 20 percent of their income by a MOH dispensation from February 17, 1994. In 1994 four hospitals (Sheba, Wolfsohn, Naharia, and Rambam) entered this process. In 1995 and 1996 all the other general hospitals were included in this plan (Shirom and Amit 1996, 51). At the beginning, public hospitals could not directly sell "extra" services, so they did it through special funds—called "infrastructure funds" or "investigation funds"—created for this purpose. Patients who bought those extra services did not pay the hospital but rather the funds. Those funds provided the services employing health-care workers on a personal contract basis, bypassing collective contracts with the unions. The funds managed considerable amounts of money, and in 1995 their annual income was considered to be some NIS 500 million.

The public-private mix presents three central forms: (1) the Sharap (acronym for "Private Medical Services"), (2) the Sharan (acronym for "Additional Medical Services"), and private facilities within the public hospitals. The *Sharap* is a system through which patients may choose their physician in a public hospital by paying an additional fee. It was traditionally applied in Hadassah hospital, and is in the process of being introduced in other hospitals too. The *Sharan* is a system by which public hospitals sell services (or accommodations) that are not covered by the NHI.[18] Hospitals may sell these services, such as routine checkups, laser treatments not covered by the law, or cosmetic treatments, to the funds (if they are interested in offering services not included in the basic "health basket"), to private insurers, or to individuals. As an example of the development of these forms of public-private mix, Shaarei Tzedek hospital's annual income from Sharap grew threefold between 1984 and 1989 (Shirom and Amit 1996).

As another way to increase their incomes, the public hospitals and the sick funds have opened private services, even private hospitals that provide profit-making services. The Sheba hospital, owned by the MOH, opened a private plastic surgery clinic and a private obstetrics ward. The Sourasky hospital, owned by the city of Tel Aviv, opened a "Center for the Treatment of Chronic Obesity," which provides services such as endocrinology, psychiatry, diet plans, surgical treatment, and plastic surgery. The Clalit and Maccabi sick funds provide private dental care, alternative medicine, and "beauty" services, such as dieticians and plastic surgery. KHC has recently received the authorization from the MOH to open a for-profit hospital (Maccabi already owns one), blurring even further the boundary between the public and the private health care systems.

More recently, the introduction of business models into public health care has both broadened and deepened. The sick funds have expanded the complementary insurance they sell in order to cover new treatments that have not been included in the public "health basket." Complementary private insurance, thus, not only offers better hotel, complementary services of relatively marginal importance (e.g., cosmetic treatments), and access to a private second opinion but also subsidizes vaccines—such as the rotavirus or the antipneumococcal vaccines and a few drugs that the public system does not provide.

The adoption of a businesslike managerial culture makes decisions on resource allocation dependent on market considerations and not on needs. Thus, resources are shifted to services and facilities that target "better" clients (younger and healthier) and not to those that really need them.

As we can appreciate, the need to contain costs had a fundamental influence on the transformations of the Israeli health care system. Two of the reasons for this need—the implosion in the cost of health care in the last three decades and the neoliberalization of societies—are common to most rich industrialized countries. The third one is specific to Israel: the growing economic costs of the Occupation, including military expenditure.

The settlement project in the Occupied Territories has been, and still is, a very expensive one that consumes resources that could have been invested in, for example, the health care system. As early as 1984 Meron Benvenisti estimated that Israel invested some 1.5 billion dollars in the settlements between 1967 and 1983. Almost twenty years later, the journalist Moti Bassok calculated that between 1967 and 2003 Israel invested some 11 billion dollars in the settlements (in S. Swirski 2005, 39).

The price of the Occupation, however, cannot be limited to the costs of the settlement project. The related security expenditure is a burden on the general budget. While combined social expenditures represent 50–51 percent of the budget, the defense budget constitutes 30 percent of the budget. This budget rose even more during the second Intifadah, reaching 32 percent in 2002, at the expense of social expenditures, which decreased to 47.7 percent (S. Swirski 2005, 90).

The security costs increase Israel's dependence on the United States. For example, when faced with the combination of growing military costs and economic recession as a consequence of the second Intifadah, Israel appealed to the U.S. government for guarantees for the issuance of Israeli government bonds abroad, as a way to finance the budget deficit. As the sociologist Shlomo Swirski accurately points out, "the American assistance did not come free of charge. In exchange for the guarantees the Israeli government made a number of commitments that would adversely affect large segments of the Israeli population" (S. Swirski 2005, 91). Among these were the commitments (1) to limit the budget deficit to no more than 2.5 percent, (2) to reduce wages in the public sector, (3) to implement changes in the pension system to a more market-driven system, (4) to privatize public companies, and (5) to reduce the allowances paid by the state to each family for every child they have.

There is a relationship between the direct and indirect costs of the Occupation and the ongoing conflict between Israelis and Palestinians, and the growing dependence on the United States, the Americanization of Israeli culture, and the deepening of the process of neoliberalization of Israeli society (Ram 2007). The Americanization of the Israeli medical establishment and the centrality of the Israeli-Palestinian conflict also help explain the lack of significant public opposition to the market-based approach of the health care system. This is surprising because, unlike many Americans, the majority of Israelis support state responsibility for a public health care system. Different surveys show this long-standing support, with some 60 percent of the population asserting that the state must be responsible for the provision of health care. However, the centrality of the Israeli-Palestinian conflict in everyday life and in Israeli politics almost guarantees that this support will not consolidate into organized collective opposition to the privatization trends.

Moreover, one of the expressions of the Americanization of Israeli society is that much of the medical establishment has adopted an American conception of health care and medicine. The Israeli universities look at the U.S. universities as a model to imitate. Israeli doctors are socialized into an American-like, biomedical approach to medicine, and many of them do part of their training in the United States. Their comfort with the structure of the U.S. health care system—one whose inequalities and treatment of the poor and uninsured would have been anathema to them thirty years ago—has made it seem quite "normal" to many Israeli physicians.

These physicians, along with many affluent Israelis, do not oppose the drift toward the privatization of the Israeli health care system. This drift, however, has not been a simple process, but a contradictory one. On one hand, the legislation of the landmark NHI law consolidated a public health care system that only the most audacious in the United States would dare to dream about: It made access to health care universal, provided health insurance to 25 percent of Israeli Palestinians who were previously uninsured, established a single-payer system to finance health care, and reduced inequalities in access to health care (Himmelstein and Woolhandler 1990). On the other hand, especially since 1997, the processes discussed above have increased inequalities in the scope and quality of health care services between those with higher incomes and those with lower ones, as well as between the young and the old. These same contradictory processes have also influenced—sometimes for the better and sometimes for the worse—the Israeli Palestinians' access to health care. While the legislation of the NHI law provided health insurance to 25 percent of those who were previously uninsured, the partial shift of the costs of health care from the public sphere to the private one deepened the long-time exclusion of Israeli Palestinians and, as we shall see in chapter 3, especially of the Bedouins.

3

The Health of Israeli Palestinians and Bedouins

Summer in the Negev: heat, dust. El Sara is one of the Negev Bedouin's unrecognized villages—the home of a few thousand Bedouins. It was not easy to get here since there are no paved roads, nor road signs. It is difficult to walk through the village, which consists of a group of ramshackle houses, because the unrelenting Negev sun makes every movement a torment. El Sara reminds me of the shantytowns in Buenos Aires known as the *villas miseria,* conglomerations of rundown houses built out of bricks, tin, and wood, with no running water or sewage, that give dubious shelter to the poor from the Argentinean provinces or from neighboring countries who have arrived in the city in search of work and better living conditions. The forty-five Bedouin unrecognized villages, home to nearly seventy-five thousand people, like the *villas miseria,* lack basic services such as electricity, running water, and sewage. There is a long-standing conflict about land ownership between the Bedouins and the state. To pressure the inhabitants in these villages to move to other towns and renounce their claims to the land, the state does not provide them basic services.

A couple of hundred meters from the buildings in El Sara, a big hole serves as a receptacle for solid waste. Since no administrative body takes care of garbage disposal here, residents have no alternative but to throw their trash in this makeshift pit. You do not have to wait too long to see rats and cockroaches scurrying and rooting through the rotting garbage, creatures which seem to run the show in El Sara, because this place has no formal status as an administrative entity according to Israeli law.

Like a person without a passport, condemned to be stateless and dependent on the kindness of whatever country will take them in, El Sara and the other unrecognized villages and their inhabitants live in limbo and their inhabitants suffer the consequences—some of the most severe of which affect their health. Public health knowledge and concerns cannot overcome systematic bureaucratic discrimination.

In El Sara, a plastic pipe carries water to a single faucet, and most residents must haul their containers to the pipe to obtain water for their households. In the summer the water is hot; during the winter nights, it sometimes freezes. Without a sewage network, residents build cesspits. Those who can afford it build concrete containers; those who cannot, dig a simple hole (Alami 2003).

In one corner of the village there is a prefabricated building: the village's clinic, powered by a generator that is turned off at night to save fuel. Without the critical basic services, it is no surprise that the health status here and in the other unrecognized villages is worse than that of any other Israeli area. The dire conditions are harder for those already suffering from illness, especially from severe illnesses, such as those of two El Sara residents, Muhammad and Zahra.

Muhammad is a thirteen-year-old boy suffering from severe chronic diarrhea who requires transparental nutrition. He is fed by a feeding pump, through a gastrostomy—a tube that is surgically placed in his stomach. Caring for the tube requires a lot of attention. To keep the opening clean, the tube must be changed frequently. The opening into the stomach also must be cleaned, and nutrients must be carefully channeled through the pump. The lack of electricity means the feeding pump must be fueled by a generator. The family received a special permit to bring a water pipe from Ksaife, but the flow is not constant, so they also store water in a container. Maintaining the meticulous hygiene that is required to keep Muhammad alive is particularly difficult under these conditions.

Zahra is a five-year-old girl suffering from cancer. Zahra receives chemotherapy and has been hospitalized frequently, both for chemotherapy and for complications of treatment. Since her immune system is suppressed, it is essential that her caregivers keep the child and her home and environment spotlessly clean. Maintaining a comfortable temperature in the stifling heat is also very important to avoid the risk of dehydration.

Zahra also receives treatment at home. The chemotherapy drugs that she receives through intravenous (IV) infusion need to be refrigerated. Because of her condition, Zahra's family and her physicians have asked that her home be connected to the electric network, but the Ministry of Internal Affairs denied her family's request. In 2005 the Association for Civil Rights and Physicians for Human Rights appealed to the Supreme Court on her behalf. The Court denied the appeal, claiming that the installation of a generator could solve the problem. The judges argued that the parents chose to live in an unrecognized village, "knowing that as a result they will not be able to get connected to basic infrastructure systems."[1]

While the stories of Muhammad and Zahra are extreme, they are not isolated cases. Nor are they the result only of the insensitivity of a handful of bureaucrats or judges. These obstacles in access to health care are the tip of the iceberg when it comes to the worsening health status of the Bedouins in the Negev, and in particular of those living in the Negev's unrecognized villages. Their eroding health is a result of Israel's unequal social structure, which combines unequal distribution of resources with discrimination based on ethnonational differences.

The Relationship between Health Care, Israeli Citizenship, and Rights

When I arrived in Israel in 1984, I was immediately granted Israeli citizenship and allowed to practice medicine without going through the kind of retraining that I would have had to undergo in almost any other country. That's because I am a Jew, and according to the Law of Return any Jew, from anywhere, has the right to become an Israeli citizen upon immigrating to Israel. The Law of Return—which was passed in 1950—elaborates a notion of Judaism based on blood. The Law of Return was legislated as an answer to the definition of Jewishness that has been used by persecutors during the Holocaust, when any person of Jewish descent, up to three generations, was considered a Jew. Legislators reasoned that if a person were Jewish enough to be sent to extermination camps, he or she was Jewish enough to be entitled to Israeli citizenship. The Law of Return was thus the expression of the will of a persecuted, excluded, and discriminated people to realize its right to self-determination and provide a haven for Jews; paradoxically, however, it has become the symbol of exclusion on the basis of a combination of religious and ethnonational origin. So I, an Argentinean Jew from an Ashkenazi background, had immediate access to Israeli citizenship.

Citizenship, of course, involves far more than the right to hold a nation's passport or the right to work and vote. As Bryan Turner argues, *citizenship* is "that set of practices (juridical, political, economic and cultural) which define[s] a person as a competent member of society, and which as a consequence shape[s] the flow of resources to persons and social groups" (Turner 1993, 2). Because of the right of return, even though neither I nor any of my family or ancestors had ever lived in Israel or Palestine, I was immediately able to gain access to education for my children and myself or my wife, if we so chose, as well as access to health care, a decent home, security. I and my children could serve in the military—which in Israel is the culminating experience of a child's transition to adulthood and establishes one as a full-fledged member of the Israeli Jewish society.

As a Jew who was familiar with the undercurrent of anti-Semitism in Argentina, it has been difficult for me to watch my adopted country discriminate against others. As Israeli society moved in a more neoliberal direction, with bonds of communal solidarity eroding, one would have thought that it would liberalize not only its economy but its immigration and citizenship policies. But the opposite has happened: The circles of exclusion that were sketched out in the Ottoman period have only been etched more deeply. And today, the Ashkenazi elite still form the inner circle. In the outer circle is the Mizrahim, a group originally excluded and then brought closer to the inner circle with the advent of the right-wing government of Menachem Begin. In the third circle are Israeli Palestinians (including the Israeli Bedouins), and in the fourth are Palestinians from the Occupied Territories.

Relations between national majorities and minorities within the same state are usually tense. Even in rich and stable countries such as Canada and Belgium, this relationship is not easy. The strength of the Separatist party in Canada and the Vlams Belang in Belgium are political expressions of this interethnic tension. But it is even greater and more problematic in Israel, where the relations between the dominant Jewish majority and the Palestinian minority have been influenced by a century of conflict, by Zionism's Eurocentrism, and by the refusal of the Palestinian leadership in the past to recognize Jews as a people. These tensions are exacerbated both by a definition of citizenship that makes it all but impossible for Israeli Palestinians to be full-fledged citizens and by a series of other discriminatory practices that exclude them from full participation in the Israeli state and ultimately affect their health.

Circles of Discrimination

Geographic or spatial segregation is a central dimension of the ethnic inequalities in Israel. Jews and Palestinians rarely live in the same city or town. Even in mixed towns (such as Jerusalem, Haifa, Acre, Lod, or Ramlah), they usually reside in different neighborhoods. Subordinate ethnic populations "are likely to reside in places characterized by limited job opportunities associated with less rewarding occupations and industries. Approximately 85% of the Arab population resided in village communities and small towns in which they were the sole inhabitants. In fact only 7 of the 101 urban localities in Israel were formally defined by the CBS as 'mixed' communities" (Semyonov and Lewin-Epstein 1992, 1102).

Spatial segregation is closely linked to Israel's discriminatory land policy. The combination of Zionism and collectivism provided the ideological grounding for a system where most of the land—including the land of Arabs who, before 1948, lived within the borders of what became the state of Israel—was publicly owned. In the 1950s most of the land in Israel was controlled by three different bodies: the state, the Office for Development (an institution created in 1952 to administrate the land that belonged to Palestinians who left or were expelled in 1948), and the Jewish National Fund, representing the Diaspora Jews. In 1960 the three bodies were united into a single administrative office: the Israel Land Administration, which controls 93 percent of the land in Israel (Yiftahel 2000).

While the Jewish National Fund owns only 17 percent of the land, it holds half of the seats on the Israel Land Administration board. This sui generis relationship between a state department and an organization that represents the Jewish people functions as a mechanism to limit Arab access to land. As a consequence since 1948 the land under Arab jurisdiction has been reduced by half, although the Israeli Palestinian population has multiplied by six. Until recently, Palestinians who were Israeli citizens could not purchase lands owned by the Jewish National Fund, so they could not purchase houses in communities built on Jewish National Fund's lands. In 1995, the Supreme Court ruled that this kind of discrimination was unacceptable. As a consequence, more than twenty right-wing Knesset members have sponsored a law decreeing that the Jewish National Fund's lands belong only to the Jewish people. If the law passes, it will override the Supreme Court's decision, and the segregation will become a "legal" fact.

Spatial segregation has also consequences on access to the labor market, since distance makes access to work opportunities in the more developed Jewish areas more difficult. Moreover, Israeli Arabs also face overt and subtle discrimination in the labor market. Israeli Arabs work mainly in those sectors that are labor intensive and pay lower salaries. Institutional discrimination is manifest in budgetary decisions, resource allocation, development policies, and, as we saw before, land policies (Semyonov and Lewin-Epstein 1994). Investment in education is lower for Palestinian citizens: They receive fewer hours per student, and their schools are more crowded (S. Swirski 2006). In Israel, where private schooling is almost nonexistent, discrimination in public investment produces deep differences in the quality of the education students receive. As a result Israeli Arabs have higher dropout rates and lower grades in the high school certification exams. For many, this closes the door to a college education.

Arab villages, towns, and cities are also allocated far less money for investment. Cities and towns have two major sources of resources: self-generated resources (city taxes from both individuals and business) and governmental monies. Arab settlements suffer from both lower taxes and lower governmental allocation. Taxes are lower not only because Israeli Palestinians are poorer than Israeli Jews, but because business activity in these communities is relatively low. As a consequence of discrimination in the ownership of land, most Palestinian localities do not have industrial areas. Direct discrimination and ethnic tensions affect the development of commercial districts. The end result is that tax-based resources in the Palestinian localities are significantly lower than those in Jewish ones.

Government investment in the Arab localities is lower than in the Jewish ones. Not only does one find less investment in education and health care but also in the development of the kind of infrastructure needed to support decent hygiene and high-tech health services. The roads in the Arab settlements are in much worse condition than those in the Jewish ones, and public transport to and from Arab cities and villages is much less developed. Not a single train stops at an Israeli Arab city because the state has not built any train stations in those cities. Moreover, buses to Arab cities and towns run much less frequently than those to Jewish localities, making it more difficult to travel to and from these settlements.

It is hardly surprising that all of this has produced significant income differences between the Jewish and the Palestinian populations. In 2003 the income of Arab men was 63 percent of that of Jewish men. Among women the gap was smaller. Because of gender discrimination, Jewish men earn more than Jewish women. Moreover, because of the patriarchal structure of Arab communities, only a small percentage of Arab women work outside the home. Those who do work are on average more educated than Jewish women as a whole. Even taking these factors into account, Arab women's income is still less (82%) of Jewish women's income. The differences in family income are even greater, since many Arab families are still "single bread-winner" families. In 2004 the Jewish average monthly family income was 11,548 NIS (some $2,500) and the Arab one was 7,513 NIS (some $1,600) (CBS 2005).

The Health of Israeli Palestinians

The exclusion and subordination of the Israeli Palestinians has a dramatic effect on their health. As Richard Wilkinson has documented, status inequality and subordination have deleterious effects on the health status of populations (Wilkinson 1996). Because they lack any public health infrastructure and face constant discrimination, Israeli Arabs, and especially the Bedouins in the Negev, suffer from poorer health and confront daunting obstacles when they try to access health care services.

The World Health Organization's Alma Ata Declaration of 1978 defined *health* as "a state of complete physical, mental and social well-being, and not merely the absence of disease or infirmity." Given this broad definition of health, excluded and discriminated groups cannot possibly enjoy a state of emotional or social well-being. Even if we adopt the more narrow definition of health as "the absence of disease," discrimination and its material consequences inevitably result in poor health. That's because poverty and lack of material resources have a deleterious effect on the health of individuals and social groups. Moreover, as Wilkinson has documented, even without severe material deprivation inequality, subordination and discrimination adversely affect health. (Wilkinson 1996). In Israel, health differences between Israeli Jews and Israeli Palestinians result from the combined impact of the discrimination and subordination of Palestinians, lower levels of social and economic resources, and more limited access to health care services.

The main health indicators reflect these differences. Infant mortality in Israel (as we saw in chapter 2) is declining, and is low in international terms. However, the gap in infant mortality between Jews and Arabs remains. Infant mortality is more than twice as high among Israeli Palestinians than among Israeli Jews.[2] Life expectancy is higher for both Jewish men and women compared with Palestinian men and women (79.1 vs. 75.0, and 82.6 vs. 78.7 accordingly).

For Palestinians, limited access to health care services aggravates the differences in health status. Israeli Arabs confront structural, economic, and cultural obstacles in accessing health care services. Primary and secondary health care services are less developed in the Arab localities. When the NGO Sikui conducted in 2004 a survey on the status of Israeli Arabs, it found that in Arab towns and cities there was a primary care clinic for every 11.8 inhabitants, while in Jewish cities and towns there was a primary care clinic for every 8.6 inhabitants. The number of specialist clinics in Jewish cities and towns is twice the number of those in Arab towns and cities.[3] Health care facilities are much less developed anywhere that Arabs live. A 1996 survey of 148 towns and villages found that almost 20 percent (28) "lacked primary health-care facilities, so that residents had to travel elsewhere to seek care" (B. Swirskiet al. 1998, 51). Even in mixed cities, investment in Jewish patients is higher than investment in Palestinian ones.

A study that compared Arab and Jew per capita investment in health in mixed cities (Jaffa, Lod, Ramalah, Haifa, Acre) found that the rate between the age-corrected, per capita cost of health care was always higher for Jews (rates between 1.2 to 1.45 higher for Jews) (Izreeli and Yalin 1999, 3).

This does not mean that the clinic in the Adjami neighborhood in Jaffa (an Arab community) was in worse condition than the clinic at Givat Hatmarim (a Jewish community) were I worked, but that Jewish patients used more hospital and specialists services than Israeli Palestinians. Higher use is related both to different conceptions about the advantages or disadvantages of biomedicine and to the fact that Arab patients have to overcome language barriers. As many U.S. studies have shown, doctors tend to take the requests of patients with whom they are culturally similar far more seriously.

The gap in health care services between Israeli Jews and Israeli Arabs improved after the legislation of the NHI law. The implementation of the NHI law improved services in Arab settlements and as a consequence also access to health care. The improvement, however, was a tangential result of the sick funds' interest in attracting a relatively young population rather than the consequence of either planning or a more equitable distribution of resources.

Health care services in Israel are more accessible to Jews than to Palestinians. This fact is confirmed by considering the costs of care per insured for both groups. The mean cost of ambulatory care per insured is more than twice among Jews than among Arabs for all age groups.[4] This does not mean that once having accessed health care services, expenditures in Jewish patients are higher than in Arab ones. The mean cost of care among the users of both populations is not significantly different. The main reason for the gap, then, is the difference in the tendency to use health care services. Research shows that after controlling for variables such as "age, gender, chronic conditions, income and settlement size, Jews are 2.4 times more likely to use ambulatory care than Arabs" (Shmueli 2005). The cost for in-care services is 50 percent higher for the Jewish population than for the Israeli Palestinians,[5] the difference stemming from the fact that Jews are 1.3 times more likely than Arabs to be hospitalized (there is no significant difference in the adjusted inpatient costs per user).[6]

The fact that Israeli Palestinians use fewer health services reflects their inability to overcome obstacles in access due to a combination of structural, economic, and cultural factors. As they try to access health care services, Israeli Palestinians must cope with geographic barriers, economic constraints, and language barriers, since, as Amir Shmueli points out, "most of the facilities are operated by Jewish staff and some are located in Jewish areas" (Shmueli 2005).[7] Israeli Arabs must sometimes travel an hour each way to the nearest Jewish city, losing work and having to pay for transport costs.

Economic constraints include not only the cost of travel but also the fact that poorer people have a harder time paying copayments for health care. Several surveys show that more than a third of Israeli Palestinians do not take all the medicines their physicians prescribe because of their cost (Gross et al. 2007). Ethnonational and language differences between providers and users of services—like dissimilar conceptions of disease and health—represent an additional barrier, especially for elderly patients. While in the primary care clinics in the Arab towns and villages most doctors and nurses are Israeli Palestinians, the same is not true for specialists' clinics. Most specialist clinics are located in Jewish settlements. Most doctors and nurses at these facilities, and all the administrative personnel, are Jewish. So if a Palestinian patient who lives in Sahnin has severe asthma or diabetes, he or she will have to travel as much as twenty to thirty miles to get to a specialists' clinic or hospital in Haifa. Once there, they will have to reveal intimate details and describe physical symptoms in a language that is not their mother tongue. While these are not insurmountable barriers, they do make access to health care more difficult for Israeli Palestinians than for Israeli Jews, and this difference reflects itself in different rates of utilization of health care services.

In sum, even though the situation of Israeli Palestinians partially improved since the legislation of the NHI law in 1994, institutional discrimination, economic constraints, geographic and language barriers, and dissimilar conceptions about health and disease all combine to limit Israeli Palestinians' access to health care services. Among Israeli Palestinians, the Bedouins in the Negev are the most excluded social group.

The Bedouins in the Negev

Before the establishment of Israel in 1948, some 70,000 Bedouins lived in the Negev area, Israel's southern desert region, most of them in the north and northwest areas. Many of them left or were expelled during the war. As part of the government settlement policy in the Negev, those who stayed were moved to the northeast area of the Negev, the Sayag.

The Bedouins protested the loss of cultivable lands and even engaged in violent confrontations with the army. The protests of left-wing parties notwithstanding, the government did not modify its policy, which denied the Bedouins' right to the lands in which they had lived for centuries. In his answer to a letter from Knesset Member (MK) Emil Habibi who requested to return the Bedouins to their lands, Ben Gurion wrote that the Bedouin tribes freely signed an agreement forsaking their lands and, in return, received financial compensation. Ben Gurion added that the government decided to transfer them for security reasons (in Porat 1993, 134–135). Ben Gurion's claim contradicted Bedouins' claims, and the land conflict between the government and the Bedouins continues to this day.

As part of the governments' land policies, seven state-planned towns were erected in the Negev, and the state pressured the Bedouins to move to these towns. Today, approximately half of the Bedouins live in these seven state-planned towns. The other half—an estimated 60,000 people divided into approximately thirty tribes—has remained in their native lands, in settlement clusters scattered over the Negev. The state refuses to recognize their right to those lands. To pressure Bedouins to move to the state-planned towns, the government refuses to recognize those villages and to provide them with basic services such as electricity, water, and sewage.

The Bedouin make up a quarter of the Negev population (Ministry of Interior 2005). In 2003 the Bedouin population in the Negev was 135,400, with 87,000 in the recognized towns and the rest in the unrecognized villages. Total fertility rates for the Arab Bedouin are among the highest worldwide: 9.0 (per woman) compared with 2.69 for the Negev's Jewish population in 2003 (CBS 2005; Shoam-Vardi 2004). Almost 60 percent of the Bedouin population is younger than fifteen years, compared with 35–37 percent among the Jewish population (Borkan et al. 2000).

As a consequence of the governments' policies, much of the Negev has been turned into agricultural, industrial, and urban development areas and closed military zones, and the land available for the Bedouin has continuously decreased (Lewando-Hundt et al. 2001). It has become increasingly difficult for the Bedouin to maintain a way of life based on agriculture and on enlarged, patriarchal families. For many Bedouins, loss of their livelihood has forced them to enter the labor market as skilled and unskilled workers. Wage labor first supplemented, then successively replaced, herding and agriculture as means of livelihood (Pessate-Schubert 2003;

Lewando-Hundt et al. 2001). By and large, the Bedouin of the Negev are undergoing a rapid economic, social, and cultural transition that involves partial or complete loss of their nomadic heritage as well as the breakdown of tribal social structures (Pessate-Schubert 2003; Borkan et al. 2000).[8]

The Negev's Bedouins lack some of the basic rights enjoyed by other Israelis including the right to an unmediated relation with state institutions and the right to elect their local authorities (S. Swirski 2006). Unlike all other Israeli citizens, the relationship between the Bedouins and state institutions is not a direct one, but is mediated by a special office: the Office for Bedouin Development. Their situation is similar to that of Native Americans in the United States, where a special institution—the Bureau of Indian Affairs—manages their affairs: lands, educational services, infrastructure, and agriculture.

The Office for Bedouin Development is part of the Israel Land Administration. Established in 1986, after the transfer of Bedouins to Ksaife and Arouar, its original goal was to deal with the Bedouin land claims. Gradually, it became the government Office for Bedouin Affairs. This Office is in charge of planning and development in the seven recognized towns, of the planning of future towns, assigning land for public buildings and agricultural use, and establishing quotas of drinking water. The Office is also a partner in decisions about the placement of health care services in the Bedouin settlements.

Until recently, the Bedouins—unlike other Israeli citizens—had no autonomous institutions, and even today there are many who do not enjoy the right to elect their local authorities. Before the establishment of the permanent recognized settlements, the Bedouins were under the sphere of the military government or special ministerial committees. Many years after moving to the permanent settlements, they were subordinated to the authority of Jewish functionaries appointed to the local government by the Ministry of Internal Affairs. For many years, only two of the towns had councils elected by the residents. Only in 2000, after an appeal to the Supreme Court, were local elections held in five of the seven permanent recognized towns (Hura, Lakia, Ksaife, Arouar, and Segev Shalom). In the unrecognized villages there is still no recognized local government. Thus, it is hard not to credit some Bedouins' claim that they should have "no taxation without representation." In the local council of the settlement

Bnei Shimon, for example, Bedouins must pay taxes to the local council but do not have the right to vote (S. Swirksi 2006).

The Bedouins have half the per capita income, twice as many children, and half the living space of the average Israeli. Their rates of unemployment are the highest in Israel. The Bedouins record the weakest socioeconomic indicators among Israeli citizens. In 2000, their average annual family income was 4,925 NIS ($1,070) compared with an Israeli average of 10,988 NIS ($2,390) (Al-Krenawi et al. 2004). In a survey of Bedouin women, 36 percent stated their husband was unemployed, and none of the women worked outside the domestic sphere (Cwikel and Barak 2003). The average income of Bedouin workers is 30–40 percent lower than the average income in the neighboring, mostly Jewish, city of Beer Sheva.

The seven recognized permanent towns are already twenty years old or more. However, they are not included in the government's development plans and still lack urban infrastructure and a viable economic life. They cannot provide enough work to their inhabitants nor are they able to fund enough decent municipal services. They face several serious problems, including lack of land for development, limited budgets, poor infrastructure, a poor educational system, and poor health care services (Abu Saad et al. 1999).

The land under their control is scarce, making development difficult. While the population in those towns is 16 percent of the area around Beer Sheva, the land under their control is 0.5% of the land in the region. The unequal distribution of land is clear when we compare Bedouin and Jewish settlements. The town Dimona has 33.7 thousand inhabitants, while the Bedouin city Raat has 34.1 thousand. However, Dimona has jurisdiction over 30.6 square kilometers (sq km), 3.5 times more than Raat (8.85 sq km). The Jewish town Omer's jurisdiction is more than twice that of the Bedouin town Tel Sheva, even though its population is only half.

The income generated by the Bedouin towns is 3,368 NIS per capita, while that in the Arab towns is 3,581. In the Jewish development towns the income is 5,218, in the fifteen richest cities it is 5,262, and in the Jewish settlements in the Occupied Territories it is 6,046. The main reason for this gap is the difference in the tax base. The taxes collected in the Bedouin settlements are half that in the Arab settlements, a fifth that of the development towns, and an eighth that of the richer settlements. The Bedouin settlements are not able to generate enough funds from municipal taxes because the Bedouin population is very poor, business activity is low, and lack of land as well as governmental development policies hinder the establishment of industrial projects.

Governmental transference of funds is also discriminatory. Even the Bedouin recognized settlements have very poor municipal infrastructure and severely underdeveloped public services. The Bedouin recognized settlements have an incomplete sewage system, lower water quotas, a very poor road infrastructure, and poor public transport.

The Bedouin educational system is underfunded, and its standards lower than the average Israeli educational system. A report for the Ministry of Education indicated that the major problems that contribute to the failure of the Bedouin educational system were teachers with low pedagogical standards, a severe shortage of school buildings, poor results in the matriculation exams, high school dropout rates, and low attendance rates for women. Negev Bedouin students complete the secondary school matriculation exams at less than half the rate of their Jewish neighbors in the Negev region. Only 64 percent of potential twelfth-graders eventually attend school, and only 28 percent of this age-group receives final certificates (Al-Krenawi et al. 2004). Among women aged over twenty-two years, 50 percent had no formal education at all, 26 percent had primary education or less, and only 10 percent had finished high school (Cwikel and Barak 2003).[9]

In this context, women are discriminated against both as Bedouins and as women. As Bedouins they are excluded on an ethnonational and class basis. As women they suffer severe gender discrimination in the rigorously patriarchal Bedouin society. Bedouin society emphasizes affiliation to the extended family (*hamula*). Men strictly maintain a hierarchical, patriarchal order in which men are believed to be superior to women and the elder superior to the young. Within this structure, marriages are a vehicle used to strengthen inter- and intrafamilial bonds.[10]

Paradoxically, the loss of a livelihood based on agriculture affected Bedouin women even more than men. Within the traditional Bedouin way of life, women played an important economic role (herding, agriculture). The shift to wage labor within a still traditional patriarchal society deprived them of this economic role. Yet, they are not permitted to enter the labor force. As a result, Bedouin women are limited to unpaid reproductive labor within the domestic sphere and have become completely dependent on their male partners (Cwikel and Barak 2003; Pessate-Schubert 2003). Restricted mobility and limited access to education also limits their ability to learn the dominant languages of either Hebrew or English, which further impedes their access to the labor market (Pessate-Schubert 2003).

If the situation of the Negev Bedouins in the recognized towns is bad, the situation in the unrecognized villages is appalling. Most unrecognized villages have a population between 500 and 5,000. Homes are mostly shacks and houses with tin roofs. Since the government considers all building in those areas to be illegal, more solidly built houses face a greater risk of being demolished (even though more precarious constructions have also been destroyed). Even Zahra, the young girl struggling with cancer, still faces the risk that her house will be demolished.

As discussed earlier, the state does not provide the unrecognized villages any basic services. Unrecognized villages are not connected to electricity. There is no running water, and only a few pipes provide the water for both personal and agricultural needs. As a result, most of the residents in the unrecognized villages store water in big plastic containers. Since an average Bedouin family requires two such containers a week, they have to travel twice a week to filling points that are usually several kilometers from the village. Residents who do not own a tractor must hire one. Thus, though nominally the price of water, per cubic meter, is similar to that in other parts of the country, the actual cost is much higher (Alami 2006).

There are no paved roads leading to the unrecognized villages. They are not connected to the sewage network, nobody provides refuse disposal services, and there are no mail or telephone connections. Due to the lack of road infrastructure and public transport, people with limited mobility such as the elderly and women are trapped in the villages. Out of forty-three villages, only fifteen have elementary schools. There is not a single high school in any of the unrecognized villages. As we will see in greater detail below, health care services in the unrecognized villages are precarious and limited. Until 1994 there were no primary care facilities at all. Today, only eight villages have clinics, and most of them were opened only after a legal case went all the way to the Israeli Supreme Court in 2000. In a country that has a GDP per capita similar to Western European countries and that is proud of its technological achievements, the Bedouins in the unrecognized villages live in conditions similar to those of poor Third World countries.

People who need relatively simple home support, such as oxygen generators, cannot be treated at home and are hospitalized over and over again. This creates needless suffering for the patient, disrupts family life, and adds unnecessary medical costs. The case of Annas exemplifies the health consequences of Israeli policies in the unrecognized villages, consequences much worse for Bedouin women, subjected the a patriarchal culture. Annas is a 55-year-old woman who lives in one of the unrecognized villages. She suffers from chronic renal failure and has been on dialysis for several years. For the first few years, dialysis was done at Annas's house. Peritoneal dialysis, which can be done at home, is preferable to hemodialysis, which must be done at a hospital. In peritoneal dialysis the patient or a family member must change the dialysis bag frequently. To avoid infection, which is a potential complication of peritoneal dialysis even in the best of conditions, high standards of hygiene must be maintained.

To ensure Annas could continue her dialysis at home, her family had begun to build her a new, clean room, dedicated specifically to her health needs. Just as the room was about to be finished, the family received an order from the Ministry of Internal Affairs to stop what it deemed to be an illegal construction. As the result of lack of space, lack of water, and lack of electricity—and after several episodes of infections—home dialysis was discontinued. Now, to receive the dialysis on which her life depends, Annas must make the two hour journey four times a week to the Soroka hospital, located some twenty miles from her home. The family must bear the costs of travel. Since Bedouin women are not allowed to travel such distances alone, her husband or another male family member must travel with her, forfeiting a day's pay so that she can receive treatment.

Whadha is an old Bedouin woman who suffers from a severe respiratory disease and needs an electric oxygen generator. Her family cannot afford the costs of using a generator twenty-four hours a day, so she alternates the oxygen generator with oxygen tubes. Since she suffers from a severe respiratory needs to change the oxygen tube every four days. The cost of each tube is some thirty dollars, meaning that the monthly cost is around two hundred dollars. Patients with less severe conditions need fewer tubes per month, which lowers the total cost. However, the cost of the tubes (up to 20% of family income) still makes a considerable dent in their relatively low incomes. For a poor family living in a village without paved roads, buying oxygen tubes is very difficult. To get Whadha's tubes, someone in her family will have to travel to Raat or Beer Sheva. Whadha's condition is so serious that she suffers from frequent bouts of shortness of breath and poor oxygenation, requiring hospitalization. When she is hospitalized, she has to travel for almost an hour to a hospital in Beer Sheva. For her family to visit, the men must miss work and afford the transport costs.

Hij'ar is a two-year-old girl with Down syndrome with cardiac and pulmonary complications. Hij'ar also needs oxygen twenty-four hours a day. An oxygen generator would be the best solution, but Hij'ar's house has no electricity. The sick fund provides the family with two oxygen tubes a month (they last only a week). The family must travel thirty kilometers to get the oxygen tubes and pay some $180 a month for the six tubes that the sick fund does not subsidize. To pay for the tubes, the family must borrow money from relatives, which means they are dependent on their family. If family members don't have the money to lend, then Hij'ar won't get the oxygen and will need to be hospitalized—again adding unnecessary suffering and expense.

Health and Health Care in the Unrecognized Villages

Given these conditions, it is hardly surprising that the Bedouins in the Negev have the worst health indicators in Israel, especially the infant mortality rate. In 2003 infant mortality among Israeli Jews was 3.5 per 1,000, among Israeli Arabs 8.6, and among the Negev Bedouins 13.1. In the unrecognized villages, the infant mortality rates are more than three times the local average and about twice the average for the Israeli Arab population: 16.6 (per 1,000 live births) in 2003 compared with 5.2 among the Jewish population of the southern region and 8.2 among Israeli Arabs (CBS 2005).

The Ministry of Health attributes the relatively high infant mortality due to congenital malformations (such as malformations of the neurological system or chromosomal abnormalities) due to the fact that the Bedouins intermarry. Indeed, birth defects do occur with relative high frequency because of widely common consanguine marriage. Congenital malformations account for 43.3 percent of infant deaths, compared with 27.5 percent among the Jewish population. However, they do not explain the entire difference between the Jews' and Bedouins' infant mortality rates. Infectious diseases and factors labeled "unknown" account for 25 percent of the cases (8.7% and 15.3% compared with 5.5% and 5.5% for the Jewish population respectively) and for 57 percent of cases of late neonatal death. This suggests that socioeconomic factors also play a role in the different rates of infant mortality (Shoam-Vardi 2004). Because of—among other things—poor sanitation, poor education, and limited access to health services, Bedouin babies' average birth weight is lower than the birth weight of infants born to the local Jewish population. This contributes to higher rates of infant morbidity and mortality. Infant and child morbidity are also higher among the Bedouins. A recent study found that 90 percent of children hospitalized at Soroka district hospital are Bedouin (Dohan 2001).

While Israeli socioeconomic status is similar to that of the OECD countries, some diseases uncommon in developed countries—such as Murine typhus—are typical among the Negev Bedouins. Murine typhus is a disease known to be endemic among populations living in poverty who and exposed to rats and their fleas, and it is a common cause of febrile illness among Bedouin children (Shalev et al. 2006).[11] Diarrhea is also common among Bedouin children, and they are hospitalized for diarhea four times more than Jewish children in the Negev. The risk of hospitalization for diarrhea is even higher in the unrecognized villages (1.5 times greater for a child there than for Bedouins in the recognized towns, and 5.5 times greater than Jews). Lack of electricity, water, and the fact that they have no sewage system greatly increases the risk of diarrhea and contributes to the heightened risk of dehydration due to diarrhea. In many cases hospitalization could be avoided if these children lived in better conditions. Pediatricians working in emergency rooms are well aware that releasing a Bedouin child who is ill means sending that child back to a house without electricity and running water. For the pediatrician, hospitalization becomes the only way to provide sick Bedouin children with a temporary haven that will protect them—at least for a while. Again, family life is disrupted, the child may be frightened and anxious because they are in an alien environment, and health care costs skyrocket.

Poor environmental conditions also increase morbidity. Researchers and activists in the United States have demonstrated the relationship among racism, lower socioeconomic status, and environmental injustice. For example, industrial sites that produce toxic waste and other contaminants are often placed near residential areas where minorities or poor people live.

The Negev Bedouins—the population that faces the most discrimination in the Israeli periphery—not surpisingly confront a similar situation. The industrial area of Ramat Hovav is infamous for its polluting industries.

Ramat Hovav Industrial Park was established in the mid-1970s to concentrate many of Israel's chemical and other heavy industries in one place that was relatively far from populated areas. Factories defined as "heavy polluters" were relocated to this industrial park, situated some twelve kilometers south of Beer Sheva. Today, there are eighteen factories on the site, including the only storage area in Israel for dangerous waste. People as far away as the neighboring Beer Sheva suffer from the smell and sting of Ramat Hovav's fumes. The unrecognized villages Wadi El Naam and Wadi Limshash are the populated settlements closest to Ramat Hovav. Wadi El Naam, the largest unrecognized village, has a population of 6,000. In Wadi Limshash live some 1,000 to 1,200 people. Bedouins who live in these two villages suffer from the daily dose of pollutants: They have a higher rate of pulmonary diseases and increased hospitalization rates for chronic obstructive pulmonary disease (Kordysh et al. 2005).

The problems Bedouins face are compounded by their difficulties accessing health services. This is a problem for all Israeli Palestinians, but it is even more acute for the Bedouins in both recognized and unrecognized villages.

The implementation of the NHI law solved the problem of lack of health insurance, which was the main factor limiting Bedouin's access to health care services before 1995. Until then, an estimated 40 percent of Bedouins had no health insurance and received curative services on a fee-for-service basis from local clinics, private physicians, and the Soroka hospital. National health insurance has improved access of Bedouin families to primary care, which theoretically means they can be diagnosed and treated in a timely manner. Although all Bedouins are now eligible for membership in the sick funds and more services are ostensibly available to them (making their access to health care services better than that of more than forty million uninsured U.S. citizens), a number of factors, including poor infrastructure, lack of resources, and a lack of culturally sensitive services, still hamper their ability to get the health care they need. Israeli health officials have done no planning to meet the special needs of the Bedouin minority, nor have they made the investments that would be necessary to overcome systematic and prolonged discrimination. Thus the

Bedouins still face significant obstacles in access to health care (Morad et al. 2006). For example, in a survey on access to health care services among Bedouin women living in the unrecognized villages, almost four out of five respondents reported difficulties in accessing services. More than half of them reported lack of transport as the main barrier; a third of the women said they could not get to a doctor or clinic because of bad weather (which makes poor roads impassable). A fifth of them said they had difficulties in reaching health care services because they did not have someone to look after their children while they visited the doctor.

Obstacles in accessing health care include underdevelopment of services in the Bedouin towns and villages, economic constraints, and language barriers. Medical services are underdeveloped in the Bedouin settlements and especially so in the unrecognized villages. Most of the unrecognized villages do not have any health care services at all. Since 2000, as a result of petitions to the Supreme Court, thirteen community clinics, one mobile unit, and seven mother-and-child health clinics were opened in the unrecognized villages.[12] Nonetheless, the physical conditions are still dire: All the clinics are located in large trailers with electricity provided by generators. The absence of electricity for part of the day means that the clinics cannot keep medicines requiring refrigeration, including common medicines such as insulin used by diabetic patients. To purchase or obtain medicines that require refrigeration, patients must travel to urban centers. They then must figure out how to store the medications when they get back to villages or houses that have no electricity and thus no source of refrigeration.

Salim is a diabetic who lives in one of the unrecognized villages. He needs insulin every day. Insulin needs refrigeration. So Salim's family travels thirty kilometers each way once a week to buy it at one of the nearby towns. Since the family can afford to use a generator for only four hours a day, they thought they could freeze the insulin to keep it cold until the next day. Unfortunately this is not a good solution, because insulin should not be frozen.

In general, the supply of medication in the unrecognized villages' clinics is limited. As a participant in a focus group on health care services in the unrecognized villages said, "We come to the clinic and the staff tells us 'We don't have this medication here, go bring it from Beer Sheva [the nearest major city]. Why don't they bring it here if they bring it to Yerucham and Dimona [nearby Jewish towns]?'" (Borkan et al. 2000).

When compared with clinics in other Jewish towns and villages, the clinics in the unrecognized villages are open fewer days and for fewer hours in a day. Most of the clinics are open only in the morning and around lunchtime, and the number of medical doctors is one-third of the recommended physician-community rate.[13] In theory, there should be at least fifty physicians in the unrecognized villages. In practice, there are eight physicians in the villages and six in the clinics in the recognized towns. In thirty-eight villages, there is no medical service. Some of the villages with no primary care are relatively well populated, such as Wadi Alna'am (6,000 inhabitants) and Al Fur'a (3,700 inhabitants).

Orli Alami, in her report for Physicians for Human Rights, aptly pointed to the differences between the state of services in the unrecognized villages and services in Jewish villages and towns: "By way of comparison, Moshav Nevatim, adjacent to Alzarnug, has a population of 600, and approximately 500 files in its clinic, which is open three times a week, once in the afternoon. In Lehavim, which had a population of 3,020 in 1998, there are two clinics, each with a family physician, pediatrician and regular visits by specialists" (Alami 2003, 60–61). In all villages and many towns in Israel (whether Jewish or Arab), there are no emergency services at night, and people in need of care must travel to nearby hospitals or emergency clinics. The population of the unrecognized villages has the added problem that the Magen David (Israeli Red Cross) ambulances, lacking road infrastructure and road signs, usually do not enter the villages but wait at the main road for the patients to be brought to them.

Preventive services for the Bedouin population are better than primary care services (despite the lack of running water and electricity). There are seven Mother and Child Health (MCH) stations located in trailers adjacent to the clinics or that share a trailer between them. Opening hours are usually two mornings a week (8:30–12:30); gynecologists and pediatricians take turns and are available on average every other week. To provide preventive health care to an estimated 16,000 women of reproductive age who have an average of nine children each, however, the number of available physicians is hardly sufficient (Alami 2003). In its response to a question posed by a researcher for Physicians for Human Rights, the Regional Health Office recognized the shortfalls but claimed that "its suggestions for upgrading are repeatedly turned down by the Ministry of Health" (Gottlieb 2006).

Another critical component of preventive medicine is vaccination. In this area, national proactive policies led to a significant improvement in the percentage of coverage since the 1990s. A few years ago, a national commission was formed to improve immunization coverage among Bedouin infants in the Negev. The commission recommended the following interventions:

1. Implementation of educational, community-based programs aimed at increasing the awareness among the Bedouin population of the importance of routine immunizations.
2. Establishment of mobile immunization teams for home immunization of infants and children who were not brought to mother-and-child clinics for routine immunizations.
3. Personal interviews with every Bedouin woman after delivery on the maternity wards of the regional medical center to encourage the mother to register her infant at the local MCH clinic and to obtain information about the location of her residence so that mobile immunization teams could make a home visit if necessary.
4. Allocation of sufficient financial resources to hire adequate numbers of nursing, educational, and administrative personnel.
5. Incentive payment to attract nurses to work in MCH clinics in the Bedouin sector in the Negev.

The partial implementation of these recommendations produced a marked increase in immunization coverage and a corresponding decrease in vaccine-preventable diseases in Bedouin infants and children. Unfortunately, funding was not made available for an adequate number of MCH doctors and nurses, nor was any special incentive pay to attract public-health nurses to work in the Bedouin sector in the Negev budgeted. Nonetheless, the improvement in vaccination coverage proves that proactive policies do indeed improve health care and health status. The former is a good example of the fact that imputing the poorer health status of the Bedouins only to idiosyncratic habits (such as intermarriage and resistance to genetic counseling) is a way of "blaming the victim," whereas this intervention demonstrates that even a modest investment in improving health services results in real health benefits.

Bedouins have long insisted that distance to the clinics and lack of public transport are the major barriers to accessing health care services

(Abu Saad et al. 1999).[14] For a poor population such as the Bedouins in the unrecognized villages, traveling hinders access to health care not only because it is time consuming but because it is expensive. Copayments and user fees add to this financial burden and make health care access even more difficult.

Finally, Bedouins in the unrecognized villages—particularly Bedouin women like Whadha—face severe cultural obstacles in accessing health care. The language barrier represents a major obstacle in accessing health care and in quality of care (Borkan et al. 2000). Services are not culturally sensitive, and many health care providers are not fluent in Arabic. Focus groups found that Bedouins felt that the clinics didn't have enough Bedouin nurses and physicians and that services were delivered in a way that displayed little knowledge or sensitivity to the particular characteristics of Bedouin society (Borkan et al. 2000). Participants in focus groups emphasized that physicians rarely spoke Arabic, which made communication difficult, especially for women and the elderly. One participant expressed his frustration, asking "From where did they bring us these Russian doctors? We can't understand them and they don't understand us, but it's not [the doctors'] fault" (Borkan et al. 2000, 212).

Bedouin women, as mentioned above, especially suffer from these barriers because of their multilayered subordination. As a subordinate ethnonational group, they do not have enough services in Arabic. As a result of their gender status in an oppressive patriarchal society, most of them are not allowed to work and/or attend school, and thus they speak little or no Hebrew. When they go to a doctor, clinic, or hospital, the process of translation from Hebrew to Arabic is problematic. Most of those who serve as translators for the Bedouin women are the woman's husband or another male relative. With a husband or male relative as translator, the woman automatically forfeits any right to privacy.

Moreover, many Bedouin women are not allowed to travel alone and they are forced to seek health care services in the company of a chaperone who is usually a husband or other male relative. When clinics are only a walk away, most women walk alone. If getting to a clinic involves public transportation, they must be accompanied.[15] As another participant in the focus groups stated: "Most of the problems [with access] involve our women. They can't get to the clinics when there is no arranged transport and thus must travel far by foot. Only Allah knows who will meet the

woman on the road and convince her [to go with him] or to take her"
(Borkan et al. 2000, 212).

Distance and women's subordination combine to block women's access to health care services. In their research, Lewando-Hundt et al. (2001)
found that the more remote a woman's residence and the more her access
to health care was mediated by men, the more she was likely to under-
utilize health services. In their decisions about accessing health care services, Bedouin women have to balance medical risk against considerable
social risks (Lewando-Hundt et al. 2001; Moss 2002).

Those who posit that the Bedouin underuse health care services because
they are simply unaware of the importance of health care are once again
blaming the victim. Bedouins in the unrecognized villages are perfectly
aware of the importance of health care services (Borkan et al. 2000; Cwikel
and Barak 2003). They are also aware that in order to access these services,
they must overcome decades of exclusion and prejudice. Participants in the
focus groups cited above expressed their concern that "the current medical
service model effectively excluded Negev Bedouin in the periphery from
receiving health care" (Borkan et al. 2000, 213).

The poor health status and the limited access to health care the Bedouin
experience are not due to "cultural backwardness." They are the result of
class domination and gender subordination structured by the Bedouins'
exclusion and complicated by internal Bedouin norms and customs. The
response of the head of the Ministry of Health's southern region to Physicians for Human Rights 2003 report on the health of the Bedouins in the
unrecognized village exemplifies the state's failure to recognize the impact
of this exclusion. The MOH senior officer (quoted in Alami 200e3, 58)
insisted that the PHR report presented a distort view of the situation and
argued that:

> In contrast to the Arab population in other Middle Eastern countries, the
> Arab population in Israel, including the Bedouin population in the unrec-
> ognized villages in the Negev, receives social benefits (just as the Jewish sec-
> tor does), including: A. Birth Benefit B. Child Benefit C. Income Support D.
> National Health Insurance...
>
> It should be noted that the infant mortality rate in the Bedouin sector in
> the Negev is lower than the infant mortality rate in any Arab country in the
> Middle East. Nonetheless, in order to reduce gaps in infant mortality rate be-
> tween the Bedouin sector and the Jewish sector in the Negev, the Ministry of

Health has been financing for the past 10 years a unique, multidisciplinary, multi-institutional program, aimed at reducing the infant mortality rate in the Bedouin sector in the Negev, with an emphasis on preventing congenital defects and hereditary diseases. The report does not stress that among the factors influencing infant mortality there are cultural factors that are not influenced by the state, such as the custom of consanguineous marriage.

This response is remarkable not just for the way it blames the victim in its final sentence, but because this senior state officer does not seem to consider Negev's Bedouins to be Israeli citizens but rather members of "the Arab population in the Middle East." With this frame of reference, this doctor can conveniently compare the health of the Negev Bedouin not with that of Israeli Jews but with Arabs who live in other Arab countries. Thus, with a clear conscience he can declare that Israeli Bedouin infant mortality is better than "infant mortality in any other Arab country in the Middle East." For this state officer the logic of exclusion preempts any knowledge of the logic of public health practices. It is difficult to imagine, for example, a highly placed U.S. public health official arguing that it's all right if American Jews health status is worse than that of American Christians because it's better than Jews in any other country. Even though racial discrimination is a long-standing problem in the United States, no U.S. health care official would argue that the health status of black Americans is better than that of black Africans, so why worry? For this public official, Bedouins are not citizens in the way Israeli Jews are; they share a blurred space in between citizens and denizens. This approach exemplifies the ways in which the structure of citizenship configures the approach of the state's agents and institutions to the Israeli Palestinians. As we will see in chapter 4, this same logic is central in structuring migrant workers' access to health care.

4

Migrant Workers

"Should we allow a baby with a fever to come to the day care center?" a Colombian woman—one of fourteen immigrants in the room—asked me in Spanish. I wasn't sure how to answer her. From a purely "medical" perspective, if our goal was to avoid spreading disease and preventing the baby from becoming sicker herself, of course we should insist that the baby stay at home. But I wasn't asked to speak for the Israeli public. I was asked this question at the end of a meeting organized by Mesila, the city center for support of migrant workers, and I was speaking to migrant women who run day care centers for the children of migrant workers. The meeting was part of a course for community activists and women who run day care centers.

Like them, I knew that parents who are migrant workers cannot take a day off to stay home with their children. Even if they are here legally, they have very limited social rights in Israeli society. In this case, as in so many, most of them were undocumented. Unlike Israeli citizens who have, by law, the right to six days off work to take care of a sick child, migrant workers, whether they arrived in Israel with or without a working visa, have no right to any time off work. If they don't go to work, they don't get paid. Many risk losing their jobs.

Dealing with the "technical" arrangements when a child is sick is stressful for all working parents. As a father of four children with our family living in Argentina, I was well aware of that. But either I or my wife could always take the day off and stay at home with our sick child. That was not an option for migrant workers who are parents. Moreover, because most of them left their countries of origins and live here far from friends and families, they have no support networks that they can turn to in an emergency. There are no grandparents, sisters, or brothers they can call to ask to watch a sick baby for the day.

Well before I attended this meeting, through my experience as a volunteer at the Physicians for Human Rights' open clinic for migrant workers, I'd become familiar with the tension between the purely "medical" considerations affecting migrant health and the specific context in which migrant workers live. If I were counseling Israeli parents, I'd tell them to keep their child home from day care or school until the child's fever was over. If that fever lasted for five days, I'd suggest the parent have a physician do a complete blood count to figure out why the fever persisted. Telling this to a migrant parent seems not only irrelevant but cruel. As I said, before, how can someone living on survival wages afford to take a day off work? To recommend a complete blood count would be to suggest a course of action that few migrant families can afford to undertake. Such a recommendation, I fear, would just make the father or mother feel guilty because they could not do the right thing to care for their child. Which is why individualistic recommendations that assume the affluence necessary to follow them don't work in this context. Thus, any solutions proposed to individual families or even institutional recommendations like those that have been proposed by groups such as Mesila, have to be complemented with political activism on a broader scale. The plight of migrant workers is yet another aspect of the Israeli health care system that demands understanding and action.

The Origins of the Migrant Problem

A number of intersecting trends caused significant numbers of migrant workers to arrive in Israel in the early 1990s. The first important trend was the creation of a dual labor market in Israel. This transformation of the Israeli economy began in the 1950s when, for the first time since the Jewish settlement of Israel, the country began to depend on more and more low-wage workers. The economic growth that occurred in Israel in the 1980s and 1990s fueled the need for migrant workers. Israel became even more dependent on migrant workers when it began to restrict Palestinians from the Occupied Territories from working in the country in the 1990s. Finally, the waves of immigration from south to north and from East Europe to the West that characterize neoliberal globalization meant that migrants in search of work saw Israel as a potential source of employment.

As early as the 1950s and 1960s, Israel began to develop a more lucrative technology and financial sector (e.g., banks like Discount and corporations such as Clal) that attracted significant investment and paid relatively high wages. Coexisting with this growing technology sector is a diminishing traditional industrial sector that produces mostly textiles; a food and labor-intensive agricultural sector; and a low-wage, unskilled service sector. Oriental Jews, Israeli Arabs, and, since 1967, Palestinians from the Occupied Territories provided a cheap workforce for this low-wage sector. As Israel has adopted more neoliberal economic policies, both economic growth and the expansion of the technology sector produce even greater reliance on services provided by cheap, unskilled labor.

David Bantram has argued that Israel's high degree of ethnic segmentation as well as its exploitation of Palestinian workers following the occupation of the West Bank and the Gaza Strip set the stage for Israel's current dependence on foreign labor (Bantram 1998). Israel's economic boom in the 1990s created a more affluent population. Between 1989 and 1994 alone, Israel's GDP grew by 30 percent. More affluent Israelis began to demand better housing, which meant more construction workers were needed as well as more services. The latter produced a demand for more domestic cleaners, as well as many more workers in restaurants and fast food.

The immigration from the former USSR also spurred the demand for foreign workers. Without having made any investment in their education and training, Israel was able to benefit from an influx of highly educated and skilled engineers, mathematicians, and physicians from the USSR. Their arrival helped to produce rapid growth in the GDP, which, in turn, increased demand for housing, education, and other goods and services. Finally, the Oslo peace process and the terrorist attacks that Hamas perpetrated within Israel limited the access of Palestinian workers to Israel and increased the demand for non-Palestinian low-skilled and unskilled labor.[1]

The Oslo agreements, and the following change in the pattern of the Israeli-Palestinian conflict, closed the Israeli labor market to thousands of Palestinians who had worked in labor-intensive sectors such as agriculture and construction. For the Israeli government and public, the motivation behind the Oslo agreements was the desire to create an even more dramatic separation between Israelis and Palestinians. As a result, the number of Palestinians who received permits to work in Israel decreased significantly (Kemp and Rajman 2007). Employers in the construction and agricultural sectors pressured the government to allow the entrance of workers from other countries who could replace the Palestinians from the Occupied Territories. This increasing demand was supplied by migrant workers from Africa, Asia, East Europe, and Latin America, who lived in regions that, in a world increasingly unequal, were on the "wrong" side of the neoliberal global economy. For these workers, Israel represented a relatively rich country that, at least in the 1990s, allowed them the kind of easy entrance they were denied in many European countries.

As a result of these combined processes, the number of migrant workers in Israel, as a percentage of the labor force, is one of the highest in the world. At its peak, in early 2000, migrant workers (estimated at more than 250,000) represented 4 percent of the Israeli population and 14 percent of its workforce. By the end of 2006, after four years of harsh persecution and deportation of undocumented migrant workers, 102,000 documented and 84,000 undocumented migrant workers remained in Israel. In 2007, migrant workers represent 35 percent of the workforce in the agricultural sector alone.[2]

Migrant workers, from many countries and different backgrounds, are not a homogeneous population. Similarly, their situation vis-à-vis the Israeli state differs, depending on whether or not they have a permit to work. Thus, they can be divided into three main groups: (1) legal, (2) illegal, and (3) formerly legal (Willen 2007). The first group comprises those workers who were recruited in their countries of origin and arrived in Israel with permits to work in those areas in need of low-paid labor. The second group includes migrants who arrived with tourist visas; that is, through the "tourist loophole" as Willen (2003) puts it. After coming into the country via this route, they have found work in the informal economy, those areas of the economy that escape state regulation and taxation. The third group of migrant workers entered the country with permits but lost their "legal" status because they remained in Israel after their permits expired or because of "illegalizing practices" at the industry or the state levels (Willen 2007).[3]

The wave of migrant workers created a new social phenomenon in Israel. While some workers remained in Israel for brief periods, many stayed for long periods of time and have become part of Israeli society. This new community (or better—communities) had needs that demanded adjustments in health care, education, and labor policy. These policy responses were strongly conditioned by the character of Israel's immigration regime[4] and the structure of Israeli citizenship[5] (Rosenhek 2000). As we said before, the Law of Return—legislated after the Holocaust, during Israel's first years as a state—embodied the historical goal of ensuring the Jewish people the right to self-determination. The law entitles Jews that immigrate to Israel the benefits of citizenship from the moment of their arrival. Thus, Jewish immigrants to Israel enjoy civil, political, and social rights upon arrival in Israel. The Law of Return, however, has not been complemented by legislation that entitled non-Jewish immigrants the benefits of residency and citizenship.[6] Israel's policy is very restrictive toward the entry and settlement of non-Jewish immigrants, and practices concerning their social and political status are highly exclusionary (Rozenhek 2003). Migrant workers, thus, may only receive temporary permits, renewable every year up to a maximum of five years. In exceptional cases—especially in the caring sector—the Minister of Internal Affairs may prolong the permit for more than five years. Migrant workers, who are considered *gestarbeiters* ("guest workers"), lack political rights, civil rights (such as freedom of association and freedom of expression), and most social rights. As Shmariahu Ben Tzur, a Knesset member for the National Religious Party expressed it in 1996, "foreign workers are employed under humiliating conditions. They are exploited. Their situation is a stain on the Israeli society" (Knesset protocols, www.knesset.gov.il, 06/11/96).

More than fifty years since the legislation of the Law of Return there is almost no path through which non-Jewish immigrants can gain access to the benefits of residence (not to mention citizenship). In 2007, for the first time since the establishment of the state, and more than ten years since migrant workers became part of Israeli society, the government approved a resolution to provide permanent resident status for children of foreign workers who have lived in Israel for at least six years. The resolution was limited to children who speak Hebrew and arrived in Israel before they were fourteen years old. Between 600 and 1,000 children and their parents, who received residence visas, benefited from this resolution. Even this resolution, which represents a minimal opening of the Israeli migration regime, attracted political opposition. Cabinet ministers from the religious party Shas voted against it, claiming that the decision endangers Israel's Jewish character. To this criticism Prime Minister Olmert responded that the resolution "does not cast a cloud over the Jewish character of the state. Rather the objection to the plan casts a cloud over the moral character of the state" (quoted in *The Jerusalem Post,* June 19, 2006).

Israeli migration law and practice prevents migrant workers from developing any semblance of a stable community. Because migrant workers cannot remain in the country for an extended period of time, they cannot develop supportive social networks to sustain and protect them in an alien and often hostile land. Deprived of these community networks, migrant workers represented little threat to Israel's existing notion of democracy and citizenship. For that reason and because the economy needed a steady supply of cheap labor, until 1996 there were few limitations on migrant workers. A few political attempts to limit the number of migrant workers allowed to enter Israel did not succeed. Minister of Labor Ora Namir, who believed that migrant workers increase unemployment, tried to reduce the number of permits available for migrant workers. She had to relent, however, under pressure from Prime Minister Yitzhak Rabin. Rabin, who wanted to limit the number of Palestinians from the Occupied Territories working in Israel, was, at the same time, sensitive to the needs of the construction and agricultural sectors. The only way to satisfy these contradictory imperatives was to increase the number of migrant workers from other countries.

The policy of granting almost unlimited entry to temporary workers began to change in 1996, and in 2001 the government adopted an aggressive policy of detention and deportation of undocumented migrants. Thus, in 2000, then Minister of Internal Affairs Natan (Anatoly) Sharansky saw in deportation the way to cope with migrant workers. When questioned in the Knesset about an imprisoned Ethiopian undocumented migrant worker who asked to be freed to care for her daughter who suffered from cancer, Sharansky answered

> [W]e checked her claims and we learned that this is not about a mother and her daughter. They are not even relatives, they are only friends. Moreover, after Ms. Kabada's detention, her friend left Israel, so there is no need for her to be cared for. Before her leaving my Office announced that we are ready to bail the imprisoned Ethiopian woman, so she will be able to take care of her sick friend. There were even voluntary organizations ready to pay her bail, but she adamantly refused to be bailed. Unfortunately, under the Israeli law we must deport this woman, but she refuses to leave. I am very worried because there are many prisoners that we should deport and they stay for months at jail…In a specific case I even conceded a prisoner temporary residency status and we transferred him to a hostel since he is very ill and the doctors said that every day in jail endangers him. But thus we created a precedent. Every imprisoned foreign worker that receives resident status for humanitarian reasons creates a precedent that can be used by thousands and hundred thousands in order to appeal to the Supreme Court. This is the reason that we look for ways to make deportation easier.

Deportation of undocumented workers was indeed made easier and more "effective" with the creation of the Immigration Police in 2002, which in its first two years arrested and deported thousands of people (Kemp and Reichman 2004).

The aggressive deportation policy dismantled the long established Latino and African communities in Israel (Alexander 2007). In 2002, 4,000 undocumented migrant workers were deported, the number rose to 21,000 in 2003, and 15,700 in 2004. As a result of the deportation policy and the fact that many undocumented migrants left the country to avoid deportation, the number of undocumented migrants has decreased significantly (Rosenhek 2007).

The confrontation between Rabin and Namir cited above was an expression of the tension among the needs of globalized markets, the dual labor market in Israel, and the character of Israeli migration law and practice. Although policy makers had to allow migrant workers into the country, they could not countenance the absorption of non-Jewish migrant workers into Israeli society. Unfortunately, in Israel, this contradiction has been resolved through the implementation of policies that enhance the exploitation of migrant workers. The chief vehicles for this exploitation are the twin policies of "revolving doors" and "binding."

The "revolving doors" policy means that some migrant workers are expelled by the Immigration police (ejected through one door) while others are allowed to enter the country as temporary workers (through another door). With few exceptions (caregivers working with seriously ill people) the Israeli government will not renew the work permits of migrant workers who have been in the country for more than three years. Those whose permits are about to expire or who are undocumented are in danger of being deported. At the same time, through the "revolving door," new migrant workers are "imported" to fill the needs of those sectors that employ cheap, semi-skilled, and unskilled workers.[7]

Whether they are just arriving or just leaving, the terms of the employment of migrant workers are dictated by "binding arrangements." These arrangements were established in 1977, years before any significant waves of migrant workers arrived in Israel. At that time, the Ministry of Interior and Ministry of Labor agreed to grant work permits to migrant workers only if they worked for a specific employer whose name would be specified on the migrant worker's passport. If an employer wanted to hire migrant workers, it had to present a request to the Unit for Foreign Workers at the Employment Service Office, which could then authorize a temporary visa for that particular migrant worker.[8] This meant that the migrant worker in question did not receive a general work permit but rather a permit to work for the specific employer who requested the visa. Thus the employee was "bound," in effect, to that employer.

This binding agreement, combined with the revolving door policy, creates a draconian migrant labor system. Binding gives an employer almost unlimited power over workers. If an employer does not pay a worker as promised, if working conditions or housing arrangements are substandard, or if the worker becomes ill, the worker will have difficulty complaining about such conditions. Since residency is dependent on employment, all an employer has to do is fire a worker. Once an employee is fired, the employer does not have to worry about any complaint because the worker is now in violation of his or her residence permit. He or she has now been transformed into an "illegal alien" and faces arrest and deportation.

The consequences of this binding mechanism have been quite clear to state agencies. Binding subjugates migrant workers to their employers. The binding policy addresses migrant workers not as persons but as "working tools" (Rosenhek 2003). As Justice Michel Hashin wrote in an appeal against the binding policy presented to the Supreme Court by several human and workers' right organizations:

> There is no avoiding the conclusion that the foreign worker has become the employer's vassal; that the agreement binding workers to their employers has created a modern version of pseudo-slavery. In the agreement binding workers to employers, which the state itself has established and enforced, the state has pierced the ears of the foreign workers on the employers' doorposts, and shackled the workers' hands and feet to the employers who "imported" them.... Our faces should be covered with shame if we view all this and remain silent. (Hashin 2006)

Justice Hashin criticized the binding because it deprives migrant workers of the right to choose their workplace. The migrant worker is allowed to change employer only if he is "released" by his former employer.[9] Since visas are given for relatively short periods, employers must change their employees frequently. But as a consequence of the "binding," employers cannot hire a new worker until the worker whose visa has expired has left the country. This encourages employers to limit their workers' freedom, to deport them by force, "and in extreme cases even to employ man-hunters to hunt down runaways" (Rosenhek 2003).

The Ministry of Labor has been aware that employers and manpower firms exploit migrant workers, as is clear from the following statements of then Minister of Welfare and Labor, Eli Yshai (Shas party):[10] "Concerning exploitation, there is nothing worse than the exploitation of foreign workers, and I see no difference between the exploitation of a foreign worker by his employer or the exploitation of an Israeli, Jewish or non-Jewish. This is very serious and it should not occur in a democratic state, surely not in a Jewish state" (Knesset protocols, 26/6/98). Yshai, however, considered the problem to be limited to a few "rogue" companies that took advantage of the existing regulations. He thus argued that the solution to the problem of migrant workers was better supervision of companies not the elimination of the binding mechanism. He was not ready to consider that the structural reason for the exploitation of migrant workers was the immigration regime and its consequences.

In 2001, to reduce the number of new migrant workers entering the country, the government issued a regulation that allowed it to "legalize" a migrant worker who left his employer and was requested by another employer. The state made clear, however, that the aim of the new regulation was to meet the needs of the labor market and not those of migrant workers. The Ministry of Industry and Commerce claimed that "the aim of the present regulation is to solve the problem of an employer in need of workers…and not to solve the needs of a worker who wants to stay in Israel to work" (Ministry of Industry and Commerce 2004).

Workers are thus still defenseless against their employers. If a worker dares to make a claim or complaint against an employer, the employer can fire her, denounce her to the Immigration Authority, and she will most likely be deported (Rosenhek 2003). Most workers who have appealed to the courts to enforce the employment contract they had signed have been fired, instantaneously losing their legal status. The denial of the basic freedom to change workplace and the dependence on residence status for keeping one's job allows employers total power over migrant workers. The binding policy provokes situations such as employers "taking advantage of wrongful arrests of their employees (working under permit) in order to dispose of them and bring in new ones, declaring upon their arrest that they are runaways" (Rosenhek 2003). As workers lose their "legal" status, employers avoid paying them and can import a new worker to replace them. While Israel's workers rights legislation is highly progressive, migrant workers do not enjoy those rights as a result of the binding policy and lack of enforcement (Kemp and Rajman 2004).

In the past two years there appears to be some softening of the government's policy. In 2002 six human rights organizations appealed to the Supreme Court against the binding agreement. In 2006 the Supreme Court stated that this policy is opposed to basic human rights, among them the right to human dignity, the right to freedom, and the right to autonomy. The Court ordered the state to modify this policy within six months.

In the meantime, in August 2004, the government changed the binding policy in the construction sector. With the new agreement, the working visa is not issued for a specific employer but for a manpower company. The manpower company employs the migrant workers and then subcontracts the workers to those employers interested in hiring them. The manpower company is responsible for their wages, social rights, and health insurance.[11]

The current regulation, extended from construction workers to the other sectors, gives greater consideration to the issue of workers' rights. The manpower company is required to make workers aware of their rights and connect them with the officer in charge of migrant workers' rights at the Ministry of Industry and Commerce. Moreover, the building company that hires a migrant worker must pay a minimum of monthly hours, and there is better supervision over the legal minimum wage. The new arrangement, however, is still problematic. A joint report of the Hotline for Migrant Workers and the Workers' Hotline documented that, while wages are higher than under the binding policy, they are still only 87 percent of the minimum wage (Hotline for Migrant Workers and Workers' Hotline Report 2007).

While workers are now able to change employers, and even to move from one manpower company to another, this freedom is limited. The worker can leave the company only once every three months, and if he does not find another employer in a period of one month, he loses his visa. The agreement still links employment by a specific employer with legal status.[12] Moreover, manpower companies charge very high fees from the workers in order to arrange visas for them. Indeed the importation of migrant workers has become a lucrative business. In their countries of origins, companies are constantly forming to recruit workers to migrate to countries like Israel and charge them high fees to do so. In Israel manpower companies profit from selling migrant labor to Israeli firms. These businesses have little interest in protecting migrant workers by supporting change in migration policy and practice.

Migrant workers do not lack only rights in the workplace. They enjoy very limited civic rights. They have no right to freedom of political association or to publish their own publications. Undocumented migrants who have attempted to organize their communities have been expelled and their organizations closed down. Since they are not citizens, they cannot vote in national elections, nor are they allowed to participate in local elections. This is in contrast to countries such as Spain, where long-time, documented residents are allowed to vote in local elections even if they are not citizens. Finally, since most social rights in Israel are linked to citizenship, they have only limited social rights, such as the right to education. Migrants do have some work-related rights such as injury insurance, and their children have the right to attend school. They do not have rights to health care, with the exception to the right to life-saving treatment, and access to health care depends on the migrant worker's status.

Migrant Workers' Access to Health Care

As we saw in chapters 2 and 3, access to health care services in Israel is a universal entitlement for both citizens and permanent residents.[13] It is not dependent on income, workplace, or voluntary insurance. This inclusive approach to the provision of health care services paradoxically enhances the exclusion of migrant workers' access to the health care system. Since they are neither citizens nor permanent residents, they are not covered by the NHI law. Their access to health care is limited and depends on their immigration status. All migrant workers may receive certain services, such as emergency care and life-saving procedures, perinatal care, and tuberculosis (TB) treatment. If the services they need move beyond threats to life or some threats to public health, then there is a vast difference in the kinds of services and treatments documented migrant workers, undocumented migrant workers, and migrant workers' children receive.

Health care for migrant workers is a patchwork quilt that has been created in response to a series of interacting and contradictory imperatives, each of which is determined by its own internal logic (Filc and Davidovitch 2005). The primary determinant of migrant health is the structure of Israel immigration law and practice. Over the years, Israel has treated migrant workers as guest workers whose value lies in their capacity to work—and work cheaply. They are not considered as potential members of society. Because these workers function within a market economy, however, a second imperative or logic intervenes. To fulfill their potential as sources of cheap labor, Israel must provide at least a minimum level of health care for workers suffering from acute conditions who could, if treated, return to work. Combining this kind of market logic with immigration rules, means, however, that workers who suffer from serious chronic conditions and are therefore unable to work for long periods of time or to return to work at all have limited access to health care services. They depend on private health insurers that are very reluctant to pay for chronic treatments. Moreover, if they cannot work, according to the market logic they not only are no longer of any value and lose their work permits. Without work permits they cannot stay in Israel and receive treatment for their chronic condition.

Another contradictory imperative that shapes the delivery of health care services to migrant workers are the needs of the urban areas in which these workers live. Urban institutions and authorities must cope with the absorption and provision of services to all their residents, independently of their legal status. Cities must inevitably deal with the problems created by the fact that the state does not take responsibility for the provision of services to migrant workers (Alexander 2007; Kemp and Rajman 2007). Preventive health care services for pregnant migrant women and migrant workers' children, for example, are provided by the city (Lewental 2002). The needs of urban residents are also connected to the fourth determinant of migrant health—public health considerations. Public health advocates are well aware that many diseases and conditions do not respect the artificial boundaries drawn by the structure of citizenship. An Israeli identification card is no protection against contagious disease. Dealing effectively with infectious diseases and the health needs of the population as a whole requires not only specific treatment for diseases such as TB and sexually transmitted diseases (STDs) and efficient immunization programs but also access to primary care and treatment of chronic conditions.

Another competing imperative that influences the provision of migrant health services is the economics of health. From an economic point of view it is wiser to invest in prevention and ambulatory care for migrant workers, to include them in the national insurance coverage, distributing risks among a larger population, than to let their chronic conditions go untreated and then have to pay for complex procedures when such neglect leads to life-threatening situations. The management of chronic conditions such as diabetes or asthma at the primary care level is more cost-effective than the emergency management of its complications. Even private health insurers prefer financing primary care over its complications, but this is even more so for the public system. Incorporating a relatively healthy population into the public insurance scheme represents, from the point of view of health economics, a win-win situation. Finally, health care services for migrant workers are influenced by the philosophy and activism of human rights organizations, which are guided by the principle that all human beings have a right to decent and humane health care services.

During the last two decades, Israelis have been influenced by those who work in the field of human rights and who have elaborated an expanded concept of rights that does not depend on citizenship. This concept has different expressions: an idea of global citizenship that provides basic rights to every human being; the decoupling of "social citizenship" and political citizenship so that civic and social rights will not be a function of political citizenship; and a recognition of collective rights as different from political rights. The idea of a common humanity and the historically situated character of citizenship can ground the claim for universal human rights. The recognition that, as human beings, we are all valuable and vulnerable represents the basis for the claim for a universal right to health, which is especially important in the context of growing globalization and workers' migration.

Documented Migrant Workers

Until 2000, the Israeli law compelled employers to provide health care insurance for documented migrant workers. This insurance, however, was very limited. It emphasized hospitalization and stinted on primary care coverage. Nor did it cover infectious diseases, which were relatively frequent among migrant workers. The list of services covered was quite arbitrary, and most workers were not aware of the actual coverage to which they were entitled. Insurance companies found—and were allowed to utilize—easy ways of avoiding responsibility for care. Instead of covering the cost of treatment in Israel, companies could send the worker back to his/her country of origin, paying only for the price of the ticket. Companies could also claim that a certain disease was a "preexisting condition" and refuse to pay for it.

Since workers' permits are valid only for a year, health insurance had to be renewed each year. If somebody got sick in her first year and her condition was covered by insurance, the insurance company would pay for treatment until the expiration of the policy. When the policy was renewed, the disease that the worker had been treated for just a few months—or even weeks—earlier was labeled a "preexisting condition" and coverage was denied. For the insurance company, the fact that the disease had been contracted while the migrant worker was insured by the same company was irrelevant. Moreover, up to 2000, the fact that some infectious diseases were not covered by private health insurance schemes demonstrated that the government's concern for maintaining a cheap and disposable labor force without access to citizenship, took precedence over public health considerations.

This state of affairs was partially modified in 2000, with what was known as the "Foreign Workers' law."[14] In the section dedicated to health care insurance, the law mandated that employers have to provide documented migrant workers with private health insurance coverage similar to the health basket the NHI law guarantees. There are, however, two significant differences between the NHI's basket of services and that provided by private insurance companies to documented migrant workers: Private insurance does not cover either infertility treatments or chronic diseases that are not related to work. The 2000 law states that employers must pay for health insurance, but they can deduct up to 100 NIS (some $25) a month from the workers' wages. To improve transparency and facilitate access, the employer must provide each worker with a copy of his or her insurance policy translated into a language he or she can understand.

The law represented an improvement compared with the previous state of affairs. It imposed restrictions on the conduct of insurance companies and defined the basket of services migrant workers were entitled to, thus guaranteeing a minimum of coverage. The 2000 amendment was a result of increasing awareness among the professional strata at the MOH of migrants workers' health care needs and their public health implications. This increasing awareness, combined with pressure from human rights organizations and politicians who supported a universalistic conception of rights, eventually led the government to modify the law.

Even with its amendments, however, the law continues to maintain the dominant view of citizenship in Israel, by which non-Jewish migrant workers have no access to citizenship. The legislators could, for example, have chosen to extend the NHI law to cover documented migrant workers. This would have made economic sense. Since the population of migrant workers is young and generally healthy, the health tax deducted from their wages would have contributed to the financing of the overall public health care system. The utilization of existing public facilities is more cost-efficient than the subcontracting of private facilities by private insurers, and the concentration of health services for the whole population in the same public sick funds would have made the implementation of public health policies easier. However, not even such economic logic could overcome Israel's politics of exclusion, and the Knesset opted for a solution that maintains the separation between citizens and noncitizens. This perpetuates the view of migrant workers as "tools" entitled to health benefits only if those services enable them to continue working. Thus, chronic conditions not related to work are still not covered by the mandatory health insurance.

This leaves insurance companies with myriad ways to avoid covering costs by claiming that a particular condition is not related to work. The burden of proof is on the worker, who has to demonstrate that his/her condition is work related. The worker also has to demonstrate that, although ill, he can return to work. If he cannot provide such proof, he may be sent home if the insurance company wants to save money by not covering treatment in Israel or if the employer cancels the insurance policy.

Since insurance companies are guided by the profit motive (if you pay less you earn more) and migrant workers are a weak population that does not vote and has no social rights, in many cases workers still do not receive the coverage they should be getting. Despite the fact that, since the 2000 regulations, a specialist in industrial medicine must be the one to determine if a worker is able to return to work, workers still have trouble making the insurers pay for care and treatment.

Consider the example of Letizia, a migrant worker from the Philippines in her mid-forties, who had private insurance. She suffered a stroke because a blood clot from an arteriovenous fistula broke off and impacted a brain artery.[15] She was hospitalized, and as part of her treatment physicians introduced an intracranial catheter to reduce the intracranial pressure. As a consequence of her illness she was no longer able to work. She was scheduled to have the catheter removed, but the insurance company decided that instead of covering this procedure in Israel they would cover the costs of her flight back to the Philippines, to continue treatment there, an approach known as "plane ticket policy" (Adout 2002). This put the patient at risk for another stroke, for infection of the catheter, for a brain abscess and even death. But money was the determining factor, and patient safety did not take priority over saving costs.

The case of Irene O. is an extreme example of the trickiness of "preexisting" conditions mentioned above. Irene O. was insured by an insurance agent on January 7, 2007. Two days later, she felt sick and was checked by a physician. On January 12 she was hospitalized because of pneumonia. The insurance company claimed that Irene's papers arrived at the company on January 9 after she had been checked by a physician and denied paying Irene's hospitalization costs because her disease was preexisting (even though pneumonia is an acute and not a chronic condition). Irene's story may sound familiar to readers in the United States, where health care insurance is both private and linked to the workplace and denials of coverage due to so-called preexisting conditions are common. In Israel, however, citizens and permanent residents enjoy full health care coverage, and only migrant workers confront such a situation.

While the new law includes mechanisms for appealing the decision of insurance companies and provides the insured with more protection against arbitrary decisions than they had before, appealing such decisions takes time and resources that sick migrant workers usually do not have.[16]

The "binding" policy and the fact that the migrant workers' visa is only a working permit exacerbate the problem migrant workers' have accessing health care. The insurance policy belongs not to the worker but to the employer (his direct employer or the manpower company), who can cancel the coverage if the employee falls ill and is not be able to go back to work. For their part, insurance companies can refuse to renew the workers' insurance. Without health insurance the employee cannot renew his working permit and loses his "documented" status. The worker is thus caught in a web of catch-22s from which it is difficult to escape.

Undocumented Migrant Workers

If documented workers have challenges, those that confront the undocumented worker are far worse. Their access to health care services is very limited. As established by the Israeli Patient's Rights Act (1996), they are entitled to lifesaving procedures and emergency treatment.[17] However, emergency hospitalization is not free in Israel. Since hospitals will not be reimbursed for the costs of treatment provided to uninsured undocumented workers, hospitals may try to collect payment from patients. Hospitalization costs for nonresidents are approximately $600 per day. Few undocumented workers can afford such costs. Hospitalization debts quickly become "bad debts" that cannot be collected from the patients.

As a consequence, some hospital administrators try to avoid providing services to undocumented migrant workers. Clerks who greet patients in the admission office at the emergency room will often hint that payment should be arranged, and they will not clarify that the right to receive emergency treatment is not dependent on one's ability to pay. Moreover, there is pressure on the medical staff in the emergency room and wards to limit the hospitalization of undocumented migrant workers to life-threatening conditions. This is possible because the Patient's Rights Act does not specify which conditions are considered an "emergency."

Undocumented workers do have access to perinatal and postnatal preventive care at the mother-and-child clinics, including "well baby" check-ups and immunizations. The cost of hospitalization for birth is supposed to be covered by the National Insurance Institute even if the mother is not legally employed, provided she has worked for more than six months prior to delivery. In practice, however, hospitalization costs are covered only when the employer has paid National Insurance fees, which is not always the case for undocumented workers. Until 2003, undocumented migrant workers were entitled to treatment in case of work accidents, provided that the employer paid the National Insurance fees. However, an amendment, which was part of the deportation policy, excluded undocumented workers from receiving such benefits.

Undocumented migrant workers have access to treatment for special conditions, such as human immunodeficiency virus (HIV) for pregnant women who are HIV-carriers, TB, and STDs. Treatment for STDs is provided in clinics managed by the MOH, with the cooperation of local municipalities (in Tel Aviv and Haifa) and NGOs (especially Physicians for Human Rights–Israel [PHR]). The MOH's decision to provide free treatment to STD carriers regardless of legal status (in clear opposition to the government's approach to migrant workers) stems from a concern for public health—the desire to control the spreading of STDs among the population as a whole—not from any genuine preoccupation for the health status of undocumented migrant workers.

The ambivalent attitudes of the MOH are evident in its proposal, in 2000 and again in 2005, that PHR use its Open Clinic (or open a new one with government funds) to treat migrant workers with TB. The MOH was even prepared to pay for the treatment. It refused, however, to directly and openly treat migrant workers in government facilities because to do so, the MOH feared, would blur the boundaries between Israelis and migrant workers. That the government was willing to embark on such a project underscores that its commitment to an exclusionary definition of Israeli citizenship, rather than lack of funds, is the main reason for the exclusion of undocumented workers from health care services.

Undocumented workers have an almost total lack of access to primary and secondary care as well as to elective hospitalization. With the exceptions mentioned above, the public health care system is closed to them, and poverty deprives them of access to private clinics and medical centers. Their only real alternatives for treatment are cheaper hospitals and medical centers in East Jerusalem or clinics managed by NGOs: PHR Open Clinic and the Israel Association (IMA) clinic in Tel Aviv. The PHR Open Clinic offers a limited scope of primary and secondary care services at little or no cost. Working in cooperation with the Ichilov hospital, owned by the city of Tel Aviv, it provides a limited number of laboratory tests and medical imaging at relatively low cost. However, the Open Clinic is not capable of addressing the undocumented migrant workers' full range of health care needs or providing continuity of caring and treatment, which are basic in primary care. In September 2008 the IMA opened a clinic operated by voluntary physicians and partially financed by the MOH, which offers primary care treatment for refugees, asylum seekers, and migrant workers.

Migrant workers' exclusion, however, does not only limit their access to health care services. Even when they do access such services, like in the case of PHR's or the IMA's clinics, their lack of a legal claim to treatment increases the asymmetry of the medical encounter. This asymmetry is inherent in any encounter between a person who is ill and the professional(s) whom he asks for help. In my experience with Israeli patients, the fact that they know they are entitled to treatment functions to buffer the asymmetric distribution of power in the medical encounter. As I treat patients at the Open Clinic, on the other hand, I am reminded of my experience as a medical student at a hospital in a poor suburb of Buenos Aires. There, patients felt we were doing them a favor by graciously granting them our medical presence. They felt constrained to be "good patients" who behaved politely and did not complain if they felt they were poorly treated either medically or personally. When treatment is perceived to be a "favor" without a right that grounds the claim, patients perceive no freedom to ask for detailed information about their condition, make demands, or express their lack of satisfaction with the treatment offered.

Language barriers, previous patterns of use of health care services, and fear of being detected by immigration authorities make access to health care even more difficult. While many migrant workers and asylum seekers are fluent in English or French, those coming from China, Eastern Europe, or South America find serious difficulties in explaining themselves, making access to treatment very problematic. Cultural differences between Israel and the countries of origin in the ways health care is provided or understood represents another obstacle. However, the main obstacle is fear of deportation. Since the implementation of the deportation policy, migrants fear any contact with any authority—no matter how well intentioned that person may appear. Thus, the number of visitors at the Open Clinic decreased for several years after the hardening of the deportation policy, until it rebounded as a consequence of the arrival of African refugees in Israel in 2007. While the Immigration Police are not allowed to arrest people at the Clinic, they often patrol in nearby areas. The deportation program was announced in September 2002 and initiated soon afterward. Not surprisingly, when one compares the number of new visits to the PHR clinic between June–October 2002 and June–October 2003, the number of new visits went down from 1,092 to 797 (more than a 25% decrease), and the number of total visits went down from 2,404 to 2,033 (a 17% decrease).

Children

Most migrant workers in Israel live without their families because work permits are issued only for relatively short periods. Israeli immigration law and practice does not permit the reunification of non-Jewish families, and the cost of living in Israel is relatively high. In 1995, Ora Namir, Minister for Welfare and Labor in Rabin's government, said that "we, jointly with the Ministry of Internal Affairs, do all that the law allows us to do in order not to let [migrant workers'] families arrive in Israel, since this is against our policy. I want to believe that what I hope will occur, that the migrant workers' phenomenon will be a temporary one" (Knesset protocols, June 21, 1995).[18]

However, some undocumented migrant workers—mostly from Africa, South-America, and the Philippines—have brought their children with them. Others have children who were born in Israel. More recently, some children have arrived as asylum seekers or were born in Israel to asylum seekers. Their undocumented status, and their consequent fear of authority, makes it difficult to precisely determine the number of migrant workers' children. Some estimates suggest they number between 1,500 and 2000. This estimate is based on the number of children who receive services provided by the Tel Aviv municipality and our knowledge that there are children who are not registered at all. There are also some families living outside Tel Aviv (mostly in its periphery, Jerusalem and Eilat).[19]

The situation of migrant workers' children is slightly better than that of adult migrant workers, because they are protected by the United Nations (UN) Convention on the Rights of the Child. The Convention declares that the rights of children are to be respected "without discrimination of any kind, irrespective of the child's or his or her parent's or legal guardian's race, color, sex, language, religion, political or other opinion, national, ethnic or social origin, property, disability, birth or other status" (United Nations 1989). Article 24 of the Convention specifically recognizes "the right of the child to the enjoyment of the highest attainable standard of health and to facilities for the treatment of illness and rehabilitation of health. States Parties shall strive to ensure that no child is deprived of his or her right of access to such health care services" (United Nations 1989).

Israeli education law also covers migrant workers' children. The law requires that any child over five years of age who has lived in Israel for three months be enrolled in an educational institution. The municipality of Tel Aviv and a number of schools in Tel Aviv have made serious efforts to include these children. However, there are still children who do not go to school because their parents' fear that any kind of registration will end in deportation. Moreover, some education authorities have had difficulties coping with children who have no legal status because their parents are reluctant to be involved in the educational process as they fear becoming visible to the authorities.

For many years in the field of health, Israel did not respect the UN Convention on the Rights of the Child. Until 2001 children's rights to health care were similar to those of their undocumented parents. Under the protection of the Patient's Rights Act, they had access to emergency medicine, to developmental and preventive health services at the mother-and-child clinics, and to the Open Clinic in Tel Aviv.[20] In an interesting instance of the interaction between a city and the state, the MOH followed Tel Aviv's lead and opened all mother-and-child clinics to the families of migrants. Before February 2001, however, children of migrant workers lacked the kind and quality of services provided to Israeli children. With the exception of a few families who had private medical insurance, migrant workers' children could not get pediatric primary care services or obtain specialist consultations, laboratory tests, medical imaging, pharmacological drugs, and hospitalization.

This situation changed in February 2001. After lobbying by human rights organizations and pressure from the public, judiciary, and some Knesset members—who threatened to pass legislation that would include migrant workers' children under the NHI law—the MOH proposed an arrangement that would provide access to health care for migrant workers' children. Tamar Guzansky from the Communist Party was one of the Knesset members (MKs) who introduced this legislation, arguing that

> [T]he UN Convention for the Rights of the Child states that...states will ensure children rights without any kind of discrimination. Article 24 states that states recognize the child's right to health and that no child will be denied access to health care services...In Israel there are hundreds of children who when sick have no doctor to consult; children who when in need of surgery must pay sums they do not have...And I ask, what kind of state we are? Can we call ourselves an enlightened state when we allow that children grow among us without medical care? (Knesset protocols, May 29, 2000)

As in the case of the documented migrant workers, the most efficient and just solution would be covering migrant workers' children under the NHI law. Rather than challenging the structure of citizenship, however, the MOH implemented a special agreement with one of the sick funds. Meuhedet—the sick fund that resulted from the union of the General Zionists' and the Farmer Union's sick funds—agreed to provide health care services to the children of migrant workers independent of their legal status. Any child of migrant workers who resides in Israel for at least six months is entitled to be insured by the sick fund. The sick fund cannot refuse to enlist a child because of his medical condition. Migrant workers pay a fee of about forty dollars for each of the first two children, with no added charge for the third or more children. This fee gives the children access to a health basket similar to the one guaranteed by the NHI law. Children must reside in Israel for six months before they are eligible for the health plan, and for another six months they are entitled only to ambulatory care and emergency medicine. Moreover, children who were not born in Israel are insured but are not covered for preexisting conditions.

Again, this new regulation represented an improvement. Many children suffering from chronic conditions are now entitled to full health care coverage. For these children and their families, the new regulation represented significant progress. The arrangement, however, does not come close to the coverage children would have under the NHI law. Instead, the 2001 regulation represents a form of voluntary health care insurance. Children whose parents do not register them or who cannot meet the payments are not be entitled to services. This is in contrast to Israeli children, who under the NHI law are entitled to services whether or not their parents pay the health tax.

The difference is not only theoretical. By 2002 only 800 children (from an estimated—then—of 3,000 to 4,000) were insured (Adout 2002). The lack of success in reaching all migrant workers' children occurred even though Meuhedet spared no effort in facilitating registration and in the provision of services. The sick fund even waived the six months' waiting period for covering hospitalization.

How do we explain the participation of such a low number of children? First, the fee was relatively high for migrant workers who often earn less than minimum wage. A family with two children earning the minimum wage pays 5 percent of their income. An Israeli family that earns a similar income pays the same sum, but receives insurance not only for their children but for the parents too. A second reason is the fear that registration will make migrant workers more visible to the immigration authorities. A third factor is familiarity: There is a relationship between country of origin and willingness to register. Migrant workers coming from countries with public health care insurance are more prone to enlist their children in the insurance scheme. Those who are less familiar with public health care programs do not trust a program where you pay "here and now" for the promise of receiving health care coverage in an uncertain future (Adout 2002). Furthermore, some families, like the parents of Alejandro,[21] whom we met earlier, did make an effort to register and pay for private insurance. However, when he was diagnosed as suffering from avascular necrosis of the hip and was in need of surgery in order to walk, they discovered that the insurance company refused to cover the medical costs. After such a bad experience with an insurance company, they refused to have another one (Adout 2002). The relatively low number of insured children means that the system implemented by the MOH does not achieve the goal established by the UN Convention on the Rights of the Child: to guarantee all children, regardless of their or their parents' status, access to health care services.

In order to achieve the goal stated by the Convention, the Minister of Health should have made use of the prerogative the NHI law confers on him and included in it all the migrant workers' children. The approved arrangement, however, excludes those children whose parents did not enlist in the insurance program. This, in turn, may cause delays in the diagnosis and treatment of those children, which represents a potential threat to the health of the population as a whole. What is worse, the new arrangement is inefficient from an economic point of view. Uninsured children are at higher risk of needing more sophisticated and expensive treatment as a result of the delay in diagnosis and postponed treatment. Moreover, it puts an unnecessary financial burden on the Meuhedet sick fund because the plan favors "moral hazard": Families with sicker children will purchase insurance, while families with healthy children will refrain from doing so.

HIV/AIDS Patients

The approach to the follow-up and treatment of migrant workers with the HIV virus or acquired immunodeficiency syndrome (AIDS) illustrates the ways in which the five contradictory logics described above interact to mold health policies toward migrant workers.

In Israel there are relatively few people who are HIV carriers or who suffer from AIDS. Public health specialists working with PHR-Israel estimate that among all migrant workers, refugees, and asylum seekers there are only several dozen HIV/AIDS carriers and patients. From a public health perspective, there is a clear interest in testing, monitoring, and treating these people. Migrant workers, like any Israeli citizen, can approach any of the AIDS centers functioning in every major general hospital, for diagnosis and monitoring. Diagnosis is free and anonymous. However, while access is free at the point of entrance to the medical facility, undocumented migrant workers still face significant obstacles—such as discrimination and fear of expulsion by the Immigration Police—that limit their access to testing.

Most of the diagnosed HIV/AIDS carriers among migrant workers and refugees are monitored at the AIDS centers. The carriers are supposed to undergo periodic routine tests at the hospital clinics and are referred for additional tests and, if necessary, given prescriptions. From a public health perspective, follow-up should be free of charge to increase compliance. It is indeed free for all people covered by the NHI law. Migrant workers, who are not included under the law, must pay for follow-up tests. The cost of the follow-up tests (viral load and CD4) according to the Ministry of Health pricelist is approximately $600. The cost of the tests at Ichilov hospital, under the terms of the special arrangement with PHR-Israel and the Israel AIDS Task Force, has been cut to half this level—$300. This is still a significant sum. Not all patients can meet this payment on an ongoing basis, even though they are aware that the test may improve their chances of receiving the desired treatment. Their reluctance is increased by the fact that there is no automatic connection between payment for the test and actual receipt of treatment. Some patients who have dropped out of monitoring have told us that they could not afford the fees for the tests.

Efforts to both contain costs and constrain immigration limit free treatment for HIV/AIDS to undocumented migrant women during pregnancy and the first six months following birth and for the newborn of HIV carriers.[22] This restriction leads to some irrational and—from the public health point of view—dangerous situations. For example, one of the patients at our clinic told us a disturbing story: During the six months she received medication for HIV/AIDS from the state, she shared the medications with her husband, who is also a carrier and was unable to secure treatment. Needless to say, if the treatments were cut in half because two people shared them, they would lose their effectiveness.

To make matters worse, some health officials have used the spread of HIV/AIDS to fuel xenophobic fears among the Israeli population. Eliahu Matza, Minister of Health in 1996–1999, suggested that "the foreign population is the source of dissemination of AIDS in Israel" (quoted in Rosenhek 2007).

The Israel AIDS Task Force—an NGO active in the protection of the rights of people with HIV/AIDS—succeeded in securing the drug "cocktail," or some of the constituent drugs, for a substantial number of patients.[23] They managed to do so by using "leftovers" from Israeli patients who had switched to more advanced treatments. Hospitals also contribute small and restricted surpluses of the drugs to the Task Force, and uninsured patients have occasionally been included in clinical trials, providing a temporary supply of drugs from companies sponsoring the research.[24]

All these solutions, however, are both temporary and partial. Migrant workers cannot cope with the long-term costs of treatment. The cost of the basic drug treatment for HIV/AIDS is at least 5,000 NIS a month—usually much more than the monthly wage of migrant workers, even of those able to work on a full-time basis. Patients cannot cover any or all of these costs by themselves. Carriers and patients also face additional expenses, such as antibiotics for preventive treatment against pneumonia or periodic vaccinations. Patients with AIDS-related complications must cope with expenses for additional drugs and treatments. Treatment with the AIDS cocktail must be given on a regular basis and with the full combination of drugs. If not, the patient may develop partial or total resistance to the treatment, severely limiting subsequent treatment options. More advanced treatments are even more expensive and harder to obtain.

In the prevention and treatment of HIV/AIDS for migrant workers there has been some progress. Public health considerations have made diagnosis free for all, and that treatment is available for pregnant women and babies. Human rights activists have managed to help some HIV carriers and AIDS patients. Lack of social rights and cost-containment imperatives, however, continue to exclude most undocumented migrants and asylum seekers from effective long-term treatment.

Asylum Seekers and Refugees

Because of its geographic proximity to Africa, Israel has become a favored destination for African refugees, who may be able to enter Israel across the Israeli–Egypt border. Between 2001 and 2006, some 4,000 asylum seekers from Congo, Eritrea, Liberia, and Darfur arrived in Israel. In 2007—especially after the Darfur massacres—their number increased significantly. Asylum seekers and refugees represent another challenge to the Israeli immigration regime.

The 1951 International Convention for the Protection of Refugees elaborated the principle of "non-refoulment." This principle establishes that a country cannot send back asylum seekers to their country of origin if they face danger to their lives. Under this principle, only the UN can determine whether and when asylum seekers and/or refugees can return to their countries of origin. The Convention, however, does not mandate individual countries to accept asylum seekers. Israel complies with the principle of "non-refoulment" but only partially recognizes asylum seekers as refugees. Israel has provided "blanket protection" to refugees—such as Liberian and Congolese refugees—who have escaped from civil wars or humanitarian catastrophes. This blanket protection allows them to stay and work in Israel until their individual petitions are heard or until they are able to return to their countries.

Recognition of individual refugee status, however, is not an easy or simple process. Of the slightly more than 4,000 asylum seekers who have asked to be recognized as refugees since 2000, only 100 have received refugee status. Those who were recognized as refugees received status as "temporary residents" that entitles them to all social rights. The status of asylum seekers, on the other hand, is similar to that of documented migrant workers: They have a permit to work but are not entitled to social services (with the exceptions already noted above: education, preventive medicine, work accidents). Since the process of receiving refugee status is a long one—that may take more than two years—and since only few of those seeking asylum will be recognized as refugees, a significant number of people live in Israel with very limited access to social services and health care. The asylum seekers' population, however, is different from that of migrant workers. Most have had traumatic experiences and carry the scars of those traumas. Their need for social services, including health care, is much more acute.

Israeli civil society has mobilized to defend the asylum seekers. Voluntary organizations, groups of students, and individual volunteers have organized to take care of the hundred of refugees who arrived in Israel in 2007. Human rights organizations that struggled for migrant workers' rights also fight to protect the rights of asylum seekers. The government reaction, on the contrary, is framed by its compliance with an exclusionary conception of citizenship, which has prevented the passage of legislation that would rationally regulate the absorption of asylum seekers. Government and state officials continue to think in exclusionary terms and try to limit as much as possible both the number of asylum seekers who enter the country and the spectrum of services to which they are entitled. Unlike undocumented workers, asylum seekers do not face the risk of deportation. But some Sudanese asylum seekers have been imprisoned because they have been accused of illegally entering the country and because their country of origin is considered an "enemy country." Moreover, many of them are housed in harsh conditions, their freedom of movement is limited, and they lack social rights.

Lauren, a 30-year-old asylum seeker from a Central African country, is a victim of this system. She flew to Israel after all her relatives were murdered. In Tel Aviv she married an asylum seeker from another African country, got pregnant, and gave birth to a baby boy. During the monitoring of her pregnancy, she was diagnosed as an HIV carrier. Three years later she began to have severe headaches and was found to be suffering from a cerebral infection common in HIV/AIDS. She was hospitalized and received antibiotic therapy. For nine months after her discharge, the hospital provided her with the cocktail treatment, but when she faced a copayment of some $400 a month, she had to stop treatment. Fortunately Lauren's son is included among the children who received permanent residency. As his mother, Lauren is entitled to temporary residence, is included under the NHI law, and is receiving treatment for her disease.

Unfortunately, however, this is not the situation for many asylum seekers. Most are not granted the status of refugee. In case of disease, their meager incomes do not allow them to undergo long and expensive treatments. For them, the combined logic of the immigration regime and health economics overcomes public health and human rights' considerations.

Contrary to former Social Welfare Minister Namir's hopes, migrant workers and refugees will not be a temporary phenomenon that will miraculously evaporate thus saving Israeli society from grappling with the problems involved in belonging to the global community. Since the various trends that created migrant workers and refugees persist, they are here to stay. In fact, the dire consequences of colonialism and neoliberal globalization in Third World countries will continue to create waves of asylum seekers and refugees. Caught within the limitations of the current immigration regime, the health system is not able to confront the health care challenges of this phenomenon.

The difficulties in access to health care services of migrant workers and asylum seekers are the expression in Israel of the hardships that victims of Western colonialism and neoliberal globalization suffer worldwide. In chapter 5 we will see the difficulties that Palestinians in the Occupied Territories, direct victims of Israeli colonialism, face in order to access health care and secure the basic conditions necessary to have a decent quality of life and employment.

The Occupation as the Ultimate Violation of the Right to Health

Ibrahim is a 28-year-old who's been suffering from chronic hepatitis for over two years. He contracted the disease in 2005, and by 2007 his condition had worsened. To treat a patient with this condition, doctors have to administer drugs such as interferon. Had he been an Israeli, whose name was Ilan Amitai, living say in Tel Aviv, he would have gotten those drugs. Unfortunately, his name is Ibrahim al Adri and he is a Palestinian living in Gaza, and the tests he needed could not be done in the Occupied Palestinian Territories (OPT) but only in an Israeli hospital. To get to that hospital, al Adri, like any other Palestinian, had to apply to the Israeli security forces for a permit to travel into Israel. When al Adri applied, the security forces denied him a permit based on unspecified "security reasons."

Walid is a 50-year-old patient who has had a recurrent cancerous tumor on his left upper eyelid. The tumor was removed several times, but it is still growing. Again, were his name Alon, and had he been an Israeli living in Jerusalem, he would have immediately been admitted for surgery. But his name is Walid Al Qanou and he also lives in Gaza. Al Qanou was scheduled for a second operation at an Israeli hospital, but just like Ibrahim al Adri, when he applied for permission to enter Israel, his request was denied. Once again, it seemed he was too much of a security risk to undergo surgery. He then approached Physicians for Human Rights with his case, and the organization appealed to the Supreme Court. The Court declined to intervene. Chances are slim that either man will ever receive the treatment he needs. The same is true of many of the other Palestinians in the Gaza Strip. Their difficulties getting to Israel had always been grave, but since 2007, when the Israelis initiated a blockade of Gaza following the escalation in violence between Israelis and Palestinians since 2005, it is almost impossible for Palestinians living in Gaza to get the high-technology medical care they need.

The prolonged military occupation of the West Bank, Gaza, and East Jerusalem and the settlement project in those territories has profoundly marked Israeli society. There is no area of society (economy, politics, judicial, culture, and ethics) that has not been influenced by the prolonged Occupation. Thus, any discussion about inclusion/exclusion to health care services in Israel must take into account the situation in the OPT. Even though Palestinians in the OPT are not formally under Israeli sovereignty, forty years of occupation means that Israel exercises de facto sovereignty in the OPT and is thus also responsible for the health status of the Palestinians as well as for their access (or lack of access) to health care services.

Israel occupied the West Bank and the Gaza Strip during the Six Days War in 1967. Following the ceasefire, Israel put the Occupied Territories under military control, establishing the military administration. With the end of the war and the beginning of the Occupation, significant sectors of the Israeli leadership and the Israeli people did not see the OPT as part of Israel and considered them as an asset that could be leveraged in future peace negotiations.[1] However, certain sectors within the Labor movement, the nationalist party Herut, and the messianic sectors within the National Religious Party saw the 1967 war as the continuation of the 1948 Independence War. For them, the final annexation of the OPT became a central aim.

This approach was paradoxically reinforced by the results of the Arab League meeting at Khartoum in 1967, and its refusal to consider any future direct negotiations or recognition of Israel. The Arab League's decision provided the more hawkish sectors within the Labor Party and the right-wing, nationalist and irredentist sectors with both time and a degree of internal legitimacy to begin the settlement project. This project combined the establishment of settlements supported by the state (as in the Jordan Valley and Golan Heights) with the state acceptance (and then support) of settlements established by the messianic nationalist religious movement "Gush Emunim" (the "Believers' Block"). The initiation of the settlement project thus became the main obstacle for a diplomatic solution of the Middle East conflict. In 1971 the Israeli government declared that Israel was ready to engage in a partial (i.e., not to the June 1967 borders) retreat (Shafir and Peled 2002).

While the Labor Party initiated the settlement process, that process gained even more momentum when the Likud party formed a government in 1977. The settlement process has continued uninterrupted since 1968. Not even during the periods of center-left coalitions (the Rabin and Barak governments 1992–1996 and 1999–2001) has it been even temporarily curtailed. The settlement movement went hand in hand with massive military presence, which increased significantly after the first Intifadah in 1988 and especially after the second uprising in September 2000.

Until 1981, the military were in charge of the administration of life in the OPT. They built an infrastructure of control that governed and regulated the life of Palestinians in the OPT. In 1981, the Israeli Ministry of Defense created the Civil Administration, which was in charge of all the civil institutions, including the health care system. The Civil Administration—which "normalized" the Israeli presence in the OPT—was a step toward the perpetuation of the Occupation. The military control of civilian affairs was essentially limited in time. The Civil Administration was an attempt to create a permanent system of management of the Palestine population in the Occupied Territories. To do this, it maintained clear differences between the Israeli settlers in the West Bank and Gaza, who were taken care of by Israeli institutions, and the Palestinians, who received services from the Civil Administration. The Civil Administration provided the institutional vehicle to build two different health care services: one for Israelis and a second, much less developed, for the Palestinians in the OPT. It also maintained the health budget for the OPT, which was separate from the Israeli health care budget (Ziv 2002). The health care system in the OPT was thus fragmented from the start and suffered from the problems that are typical in health systems in colonial societies.

The 1967–1994 Period

In 1967, when Israel took control of all civil administration in the OPT, it also took responsibility for the health care system while directly administrating a significant part of it. The health care system in the OPT was under the direction of two Israeli medical officers, one in the West Bank and the other in the Gaza Strip. This apparatus was independent of the Israeli Ministry of Health (MOH), which did not have authority over the OPT, and supervised only epidemiological developments that could endanger public health within Israel.

Health policies for the OPT became part of the overall strategy of Occupation. Israel's approach to the development of the health care system in the OPT reflected the colonialist approach to colonies' development, which is to reproduce the hierarchical relationship between the colonialists and colonized. The strategy for the health care field was concentrated mostly on public health and prevention, with only minimal investment in infrastructure and human resources. Israel's policy reproduced Palestinian dependence on the Israeli health care system.

An approach that concentrated on preventive care and the administration of existing resources would have been acceptable for a brief occupation. But as it began to be clear that Israel would not retreat in the short-term and that the occupation would be a prolonged one, the lack of development of the Palestinian health care services became problematic. It became more so as it became even clearer that for significant sectors in Israel, the occupation of the West Bank and Gaza was not a temporary situation. As the Israeli settlement project in the West Bank and the Gaza Strip thrived, there was one standard of care for the Israeli settlers, who had free access to the Israeli health care system, and a separate, substandard one for the Palestinians in the Occupied Territories.

The goal of Israel's approach to health care in the OPT was to improve public health and sustain a primary care network, while at the same time keeping investment to a minimum. In the area of public health the Israeli administration focused especially on preventive care, such as vaccinations. In the area of primary care the goal was a network that could minimally answer the needs of the Palestinian population. Investment in the OPT health care system was much lower than in Israel. The result was the lack of development of more sophisticated tertiary care services (hospitalization and sophisticated treatment) and the continuing dependence on the Israeli hospital system.

The development of the health care service was conceived as part of the Occupation apparatus, both as a way of achieving some degree of legitimacy and as a mean to punish and reward Palestinians living in the OPT (e.g., as we will see later, the health care budget was reduced during the first Intifadah). Yitzhak Sever and Yitzhak Peterburg,[2] two of the doctors who, as chief medical officers in the West Bank and Gaza Strip, were the executive authorities in the health field, confirmed, in an article published in 2002, that the three major objectives of the health care system from the point of view of the Israeli Civil Administration were (1) to provide basic health services at a low price, (2) to help the occupying forces manage the Palestinian population, and (3) to contain infectious diseases in order to prevent an epidemic which could threaten Israeli citizens (Peterburg and Sever 2002). They were aware that the health care system has a legitimating role and that it could function to diminish opposition to the occupation. "It was clear," they state, "that Israel had to care for the local populations in the territories and ensure high standards of public health and reasonable medical care... The overall goal was to keep the population satisfied and quiet, and to provide a stable, calm, and reasonable background for future negotiations that would lead to a political solution" (quoted in Barnea and Husseini 2002, 44–46).

In accord with this approach, emphasis was placed on public health and a certain level of primary care, while more expensive tertiary care was provided by Israeli hospitals on a limited scale. The development of an autonomous Palestinian health system that could provide services similar in quality and complexity to those provided by the Israeli health care system was never part of the objective (Gordon and Filc 2007). Not only was investment in infrastructure low, but there was no strategy for the development of human resources for the health care system. The OPT lacked educational and training programs in health, the establishment of medical schools was prohibited, and students from the OPT were not permitted to study in Israel (Hamdan and Defever 2003).

Israel's first priorities were the control of vaccine-preventable diseases, the implementation of a broad immunization program, and the creation of mechanisms of epidemiological surveillance (Barnea and Husseini 2002, 46). As we saw above, the goal of adopting a "public health logic" within the OPT was to prevent the outbreak of diseases in the West Bank and Gaza

Strip that could potentially put the Israeli population at risk, lead to social upheaval within the territories, and increase the political and economic cost of the occupation (Gordon and Filc 2007). Moreover, the public health approach generated epidemiological data that also contributed to the surveillance of the Palestinian population because it provided information about the development of Palestinians' settlements, population, and even behavior.

These practices, however, although a mechanism of surveillance and control, also produced positive health results. During the early 1970s, only 16 percent of deliveries in the West Bank took place at hospitals; by 1993 this figure had risen to 74.5 percent (Barnea and Husseini 2002). Hospital delivery significantly diminished the perinatal mortality rate, and the vaccination program further reduced infant mortality.

On the other hand, the lack of development of the tertiary sector made Palestinians in the OPT dependent on Israel for sophisticated treatment. Most cancer therapy, complex neurosurgery, and cardiovascular treatment were performed only in Israeli hospitals. The Civil Administration covered the referrals of those Palestinians who were members of the military government's insurance program. Premiums were deducted from wages of government employees, and those who were voluntarily insured made monthly or annual payments (Al-Haq 1993). This insurance program covered primary care and hospitalization, but each enrollee had a specific clinic to which he or she was assigned and only in emergency situations was the insured allowed to reach hospitals if they had not been sent by a primary care physician. For most Palestinians, referral costs represented a serious obstacle to access to complex health care treatment. Moreover, referrals to Israeli hospitals for the treatment of problems that required expensive treatment was subjected to budget limitations; for example, Israel financed a limited number of bone medullar transplants for Palestinians every year.

Since patients needed the approval of the Israeli secret service to enter Israel, the need to refer Palestinian patients to Israeli facilities represented an instrument of control for the Occupation forces.[3] When access was denied, collaboration with the Occupation forces became a desperate means to achieve access to health care. The relationship between "good behavior" (from the Occupier's perspective) and access to health care was one of the premises of the referral process. Dr. Ephraim Sneh, a Labor Knesset member (MK) and the head of the Civil Administration between 1985 and 1987, stated that the Civil Administration functioned as a way to coerce collaboration: "The motto was 'If you behave, you will receive; if not, you won't.'" "The policy wasn't explicit, but it was known to all the involved parties, and mentioned in internal discussions" (quoted in Barnea and Husseini 2002, 125). The Palestinians' dependence on the Israeli health care system made them vulnerable to pressure. For example, following the outbreak of the first Intifadah, the budget for referrals to Israeli hospitals was cut because the government claimed that the decrease in tax revenues did not allow it to pay for referrals. Thus, the authorization of referrals depended not on medical considerations but on the consent of the Israeli Chief Finance Officer for the Civil Administration (Ziv 2002). Indeed, it was a form of punishment that was criticized even by leading figures within the Israeli medical establishment, such as Professor Emmanuel Theodor, a leading Israeli clinician. The dependence on the Israeli health care system also reproduced a state of affairs characteristic of the colonial situation: The occupier is feared and hated but also admired and envied. Thus, many Palestinians preferred to receive treatment in Israeli facilities rather than in Palestinian ones, even when the same treatment was available within the OPT.

The desire to control was not the only reason for the underfinancing and underdevelopment of the secondary and tertiary health care sectors. The Israeli military government wanted to contain the economic costs of the Occupation, and investment in sophisticated health care services and human resources is expensive. Thus, between 1967 and 1994, the development of complex health care services was almost nil. The Palestinians' hospitals maintained only a basic level of care. Between 1967 and 1984, for example, the number of hospital beds in the OPT decreased while the population doubled (PMH 2003). Many medical areas of expertise were never established in the OPT, while other basic medical fields were only semi-functional (Gordon et al. 1993). In 1986 there were 8 physicians per 100,000 inhabitants in the OPT—less than a third of the ratio for Israel. The bed per population in the late 1980s was 1.6 per 1,000 inhabitants (compared with 6.1/1,000 in Israel), and the per capita expenditure in health was $30 compared with $350 in Israel (Rigby 1991). In 1993, the per capita health expenditure in Israel was $500, while in the OPT it was between $18 and $23 (Gordon et al. 1993, 14–15).

During the 1967–1994 period, health care services in the OPT were provided by four main sectors: (1) the Civil Administration, (2) nongovernmental organization (NGOs), (3) the United Nations Relief and Work

Agency (UNRWA), and (4) the private sector. The military government supervised and controlled the whole system. The Civil Administration provided public health services financed from tax revenue and implemented a semivoluntary insurance scheme that offered primary health care and some of the secondary and hospitalization services in the OPT and financed referral to Israeli facilities when needed (subordinated to security considerations). Participation in the system was required for all the Palestinians who worked for the Civil Administration, whether in education, health, or any other civil institution. All had their insurance fees automatically deducted from their salaries. For Palestinians working in other sectors the insurance scheme was voluntary. The estimated percentage of families covered by this health insurance program varied enormously, yet it appears that in the early 1990s reached a level of about 30 percent (Pederson and Hooper 1998).

The second sector, NGOs, was divided into a grassroots NGO sector and a charitable one. The former developed as a way of challenging the Occupation. Starting in the early 1970s, Palestinians tried to build as many independent Palestinian health care structures as possible. During the late 1970s and early 1980s an important network that delivered mostly primary health care slowly emerged. So did a network of secondary and basic hospitalization services, in the West Bank, Gaza, and East Jerusalem. This NGO sector provided 35 percent of the rural nonprofit clinics in the West Bank and 21 percent in the Gaza Strip. By 1992 this sector was responsible for over 40 percent of Palestinian hospital beds. About half of the hospital beds were located in East Jerusalem, which housed the largest and most specialized secondary and tertiary care services available for the Palestinians (Barnea and Husseini 2002).

One of the central grassroots NGOs was the Union of Palestinian Medical Relief Committees, launched in 1979. While emphasizing the centrality of primary care, it was formed to offer an alternative to the Occupation apparatus. The emergence of a network of autonomous Palestinian health care organizations shows that the health care system was not only an instrument in the hands of the military Occupation but also a field where the Occupation was challenged. With the outbreak of the first Intifadah in December 1987, the number of grassroots health care organizations grew considerably as one more way of challenging the Occupation establishment.

The charitable NGO sector operated both primary care clinics and hospitals (mostly in East Jerusalem). In the early 1990s this sector operated seventy-five clinics in seventy communities, covering 30 percent of the rural population (Barghouti and Daibes 1993).

The third sector providing health care services in the OPT was the United Nations Relief and Work Agency (UNRWA). UNRWA is the largest primary health care provider in the Gaza Strip (556,000 refugees) and also provided services for Palestinian refugees in the West Bank. UNRWA, which offers mostly integrated primary health care services, has been delivering health care services for Palestinian refugees since the early 1950s (Gordon and Filc 2007). UNRWA provided maternal and child health and family planning services as well as health services aimed to control communicable and noncommunicable diseases (UNRWA 2005). With the exception of a small hospital in Qalqyilia, UNRWA's services do not include tertiary services.

The fourth sector was the private one, which in the early 1990s consisted of clinics in the cities and in some villages in the rural sectors. A 1992 survey identified 150 private clinics in 80 rural communities (Barghouti and Daibes 1993), and provided mostly primary care services for those Palestinians who could afford their cost.

Even though the Civil Administration structured the health care system in the OPT in ways that reproduced the characteristics of colonialism, the emphasis on public health and the improvement of socioeconomic indicators during the first period of the Occupation (1967–77) did improve the health status of Palestinians. In the late 1980s, before the breakdown of the first Intifadah, health conditions in the West Bank and the Gaza Strip were better than they had been twenty years before and compared favorably with those in neighboring states (Rigby 1991). They were, however, worse than in Israel. In 1985 infant mortality in Israel was 14 per 1,000 live births, while in the OPT infant mortality was 70 per 1,000 live births (in the neighboring states of Jordan and Syria, infant mortality rates were 55 and 60 per 1,000 life births, respectively) (Rigby 1991). Comparing the OPT with other Arab countries would make sense in the early 1970s. After more than forty years of Israeli occupation, the health indicators of Palestinians in the OPT should be compared with health indicators in Israel, which as a prolonged occupier is responsible for the health status of the Palestinians.

In 1993, before the Oslo agreements, infant mortality for Palestinians in the OPT was 27 per 1,000 live births. Those figures were higher than in Israel (9/1,000 live births) but lower than in Egypt (55/1,000), Jordan

(36/1,000), and Syria (40/1,000) (Gordon et al. 1993). What accounted for the improvement in infant mortality for Palestinians between the late 1960s and the early 1990s? The better nutrition resulting from improved socioeconomic conditions in the first two decades of the Occupation, the immunization campaign, and the systematization of hospital deliveries all contributed to the reduction of infant mortality (Gordon and Filc 2007).

Infant mortality in 1989 in Israel was 9.9 deaths per 1,000 live births, and in the OPT, it was 40–50 deaths for every 1,000 live births. Life expectancy improved, too, rising from 48.0 to 69.2 between 1970 and 1993, but remaining lower than in Israel. In 1991, life expectancy for people living in the OPT was 62 years for women and 60 for men. In the same year, life expectancy in Israel was 74.6 for men and 78.1 for women.

During the first two decades of the Occupation, the improvement in Palestinians' health status thus seemed to legitimate Israel's role as occupier. This, in turn, reinforced the role of the administration by reproducing and "normalizing" the occupation.

The Oslo Accords and the Transfer of Responsibility

Following the Oslo Accords in 1993, the civil administration transferred many of its functions, including the responsibility for the Palestinian health care system, to the Palestinian Authority (PA).[4] The Oslo agreements did not put an end to the Occupation; Israel retained total military control and extended control over the Palestinian economy. In fact, Israel retained de facto sovereignty over the OPT. Nonetheless, Israel relinquished its responsibility over health care in the OPT and terminated contracts related to the hospitalization of Palestinian patients from the OPT in Israeli hospitals.

The agreement that transferred health care responsibilities from Israel to the PA was very problematic. The PA received authority, power, and responsibility for health care, but Israel did not transfer power and responsibility for some of the significant things that determine health, such as water, freedom of movement, and authority over imports. Israel kept control over movement within the West Bank and Gaza and between the West Bank and the Gaza Strip. Thus, the PA did not have the power to determine where Palestinian doctors could do specialization training. Moreover, as part of Israeli control over imports to the OPT, article 10 of the health section of

the 1995 Interim Agreement stated that "Imports of pharmaceutical prod-
ucts to the West Bank and the Gaza Strip shall be in accordance with general
arrangements concerning imports and donations, as dealt with in Annex V
(Protocol on Economic Relations)."[5] Thus, the organization of health care
in the OPT was significantly influenced by the limitations on the residents'
freedom of movement, which interfered with the organization of a coordinated referral system, and by the restrictions and control on the import
of medicines (Ziv 2002). The Palestinian leadership was torn between the
political need to increase its authority, broadening its fields of responsibility,
and the understanding that the terms of the agreement did not allow real
control over the Palestinian population's health care and needs.

The PA established a Palestinian Ministry of Health, in charge of the
provision of health care services to the Palestinian population. The Ministry of Health did not have the resources, nor perhaps the political power,
to replace the fragmented health care system (the "Civil Administration"
sector inherited from the Israeli occupation, the NGO sector, the UNRWA
facilities, and the private sector). Instead, it tried to become a regulator, co-
ordinating the different sectors of a fragmented system (Mataria et al. 2006).
Public health programs were maintained, and the new Palestinian Ministry
of Health expanded the health insurance program to include up to 53 percent of the population (PMH 2000). The primary health care sector consisted
of 619 centers, 516 in the West bank and 103 in the Gaza Strip. The Ministry
of Health ran 63 percent of these centers, the NGO sector 29 percent, and
UNRWA 8 percent (Abu Gosh et al. 2007; Daibes and Barghouti 1996).

The ratio of health personnel per population increased significantly
since the turnover of the health care sector to the PA and until the breakdown of the second Intifadah. In 2000 the health care sector workforce
was estimated at about 14,650 people (Hamdan and Defever 2003). However, except for certain professions such as pharmacists, ratios of health
personnel per population are still lower than in most of the neighboring
Arab countries (Hamdan and Defever 2003) and far lower than in Israel.
Specific areas where the system suffers from a severe shortage of adequate,
qualified personnel include cardiology, medical imaging, anesthesiology,
and nursing (Hamdan and Defever 2003).

The Palestinian Ministry of Health did not succeed in improving the
quality of secondary and particularly tertiary services, and investment in
their development decreased in the period following the second Intifadah

(Gordon and Filc 2005). The number of hospital beds per capita (1:744) continued to be lower than the per capita number of beds (1:600) recommended by the World Health Organization (WHO). The per capita governmental expenditure on health in 2000 was $30.4, much lower than the expenditure in 1996 of $42.7 (Pfeiffer 2001), and even lower than the Civil Administration per capita expenditure in 1993 of $33.8 (Barnea and Husseini 2002).[6] The per capita governmental expenditure in health was less than 30 percent of the total health expenditure, which meant that NGOs and UNRWA played increasingly significant roles. This despite that the Ministry of Health is the major employer and accounts for about 56.6 percent of the health care system's workforce (ibid). Moreover, as part of the policy of development of the health care sector that the PA adopted under the auspices of the World Bank, the private sector grew (Davidi 2000).

As a result of the legacy of the Occupation and the policies adopted by the PA, six years after the transfer of responsibility for the health care system, Palestinians in the OPT were still dependent on Israel (and also on Egypt and Jordan) for the provision of tertiary health care. Initially the Palestinian Ministry of Health maintained the situation that existed before the Oslo agreements and signed contracts with Israeli hospitals—contracts that diverted precious funds from the PA to Israel. Eventually, the PA redirected many of those patients in need of sophisticated treatment to Egypt and Jordan, where hospitalization was cheaper. However, the continuous deterioration of the Palestinian economy made referrals more and more difficult. In 1995 the PA spent over $14 million on referrals abroad. By the year 2000 it spent just over $6 million (PMH 2000).

The fact that tertiary health care was provided in other countries made Palestinians' access to complex health care service dependent on Israel's will or whims, since Israel still controlled the means of access into and out of the OPT. With the outbreak of the second Intifadah in September 2000, this dependence would have dire consequences for the health of Palestinians.

The Second Intifadah and Limitations
on Access to Health Care Services

Since the beginning of the second Intifadah[7] in September 2000, health care provision in the OPT has deteriorated. This is a result of the conflict, the resultant economic crisis in the OPT, increasing obstacles in access to health care services, and direct attacks on medical services and personnel (Ziv 2002). The Palestinian health care system is marked by the defects of a colonial system discussed above, the influence of neoliberal policies, especially under the influence of the World Bank, the failures of the PA, and the added weight of violence and increased oppression, as we will see below.

Israel's harsh restrictions on movement and direct attacks on Palestinian civil society institutions, such as NGOs, have destroyed the infrastructure on which daily life depends. The economy has deteriorated and poverty has increased, producing dire living conditions and severely restricted access to health care. Following the Passover 2000 terrorist attack to a hotel in Netanyha that killed 30 and wounded 140, Israel launched Operation "Defensive Shield," and significant areas of the West Bank were reoccupied. The health status of the Palestinians eroded as a consequence of direct attacks and increasing poverty. Simultaneously, the economic crisis in the OPT has reduced the ability of the Palestinian health care system to cope with the growing needs. This situation has been exacerbated by harsh restrictions on freedom of movement that made access to health care facilities very difficult.

The economy in the OPT suffered a serious blow as the result of the blockades and curfews, the closure of the OPT, and direct violence (Giacaman et al. 2004). In 1999, per capita GDP in the OPT was $1,850. It fell to $1,110 by 2003, and in 2005 it decreased 45 percent from its level at the beginning of the second Intifadah (World Bank 2006). As a result, unemployment and poverty increased dramatically, tripling the 1999 poverty rate.

Poverty rates in the Gaza Strip reached 75 percent before the disengagement in 2005. Since then, the situation has worsened even more. Even among the employed, poverty rates are extremely high. In 2006, the poverty rate among government employees in Gaza reached 71 percent, from a previous 35 percent (Oxfam 2007). Due to restrictions on movement of people and goods and on the transfer of revenues collected by the Israeli government on the PA's behalf, Palestinians' real personal income decreased almost 40 percent between 2000 and 2002 (World Bank 2006).

The destruction of infrastructure and the severe limitations on movement created problems in water supply and sanitation, with solid waste accumulating within cities (World Bank 2006; Morad et al. 2006). Frequent interruptions of electricity during military operations destroyed food supplies

(Giacaman et al. 2004) As a consequence, acute and chronic malnutrition increased considerably, affecting some 3 percent and 9 percent of Palestinian children in the OPT, respectively (World Bank 2004; Qouta et al. 2003). Lack of food was much more pervasive, affecting almost 40 percent of the Palestinians in the OPT, and per capita food consumption decreased 25 percent since 1998 (World Bank 2003).

Among the consequences of the economic and infrastructure crises, almost half of the children between six months and fifty-nine months (i.e., five years old) and women of childbearing age are anemic. Not only because of poverty but also because of the worsening quality of drinking water and sanitation. Diseases related to poor living conditions, such as acute diarrhea, have increased dramatically (UNRWA 2007). As a result of poor maternal conditions and poor prenatal care, the number of stillbirths increased by 58 percent in the last five years. Child mortality also increased, becoming the second leading cause of death overall (WHO 2003).

The violent conflict also had a dramatic impact on health. The second Intifadah brought an escalation in violence and increased fatalities for both Israelis and Palestinians. However, because of the unequal balance of forces, the death toll and the number of wounded among Palestinians were much higher. Between the onset of the second Intifadah in September 2000 and year 2004, 2,762 Palestinians have been killed and more than 50,000 have been injured (among them 700 children killed and more than 14,000 injured). Some 10 percent of them suffer from permanent disabilities, and many more require prolonged and complex medical treatment—which it is difficult, if not impossible, to get (Quouta et al. 2003). Between the years 2000 and 2003, the demand for blood transfusion services increased by 178 percent. In 2003, hospital emergency wards treated 749,318 injuries, an increase of 52.6 percent over the year 2000 (UNRWA 2007).

While the health status of Palestinians deteriorated and their health care needs increased, the ability of the health care system to respond to these needs diminished both because of budgetary distress and limitations on access. The 2003 annual government budget for health was $98.4 million or $26.3 per capita. In real terms it represented about half the government per capita health expenditure in 1996, which reached $42.7 (PMH 2003). As a consequence, there has been a continuing erosion of the system as well as shortages of drugs. The budgetary constraints and the impoverishment of the population brought a sharp decline in the number of people covered by the governmental health insurance program, which fell from over 53 percent in 1999 to 38 percent by 2003.

Economic hardship is not the only factor that limits Palestinians' access to health care services. The number and quality of health care providers has also been affected by the continuing conflict. Health care providers have a hard time attending continuing education programs, and students are not allowed to continue their medical or paramedical education. Not surprisingly, the OPT suffers from "brain drain" of qualified health care providers as a result of political instability and difficult economic and working conditions (Hamdan and Defever 2003).

The main factor affecting access to health care services in the OPT have been the severe restrictions on the freedom of movement. Limits on movement into Israel and within the OPT were already present in the post-Oslo era, before the outbreak of the second Intifadah. Those limits worsened significantly after October 2000, when Israel implemented a total closure of the West Bank and Gaza Strip, including denying entrance to East Jerusalem, the main provider of tertiary care for the West Bank. Internal closure that restricted movement between the West Bank and Gaza Strip, however, was the main obstacle for access to health care services.

The West Bank was dissected into northern and southern blocs (with Jerusalem and its environs in between), and then additionally divided into regions according to city-governorates: Jenin, Nablus, Ramallah, Salfeet, Jericho, Tul Karm, Qalqilya, Bethlehem, and Hebron. Each region was, in turn, divided into subregions, which may at times constitute a single village, isolated from all other villages and towns in its vicinity. By the end of 2003 there were 56 manned checkpoints in the West Bank, as well as 607 physical roadblocks that prevented the passage of motor vehicles. The techniques used to create roadblocks were varied—concrete blocks, high earth embankments, concrete walls, deep ditches, and ditches into which sewage was diverted so that they could not be crossed even on foot. By the end of 2003 there were 457 dirt piles, 94 concrete blocks, and 56 trenches (Swissa 2003). Moreover, most of the main roads in the West Bank are closed for Palestinians. Israel either totally forbids Palestinians from using the main interurban roads in the West Bank, or it drastically limits their rights to use them (limiting the use to certain hours or to drivers possessing a permit) (Lain 2004).

At times, the internal closure has been accompanied by siege (known by the euphemism "encirclement"). Israel has "encircled" districts and individual villages, cutting them off from the remaining parts of the West Bank. Until the disengagement in 2005, the Gaza Strip was dissected by the Gush Katif checkpoints into two blocs: the southern one, including Rafah and Khan Younis, and the northern bloc, which included Deir al-Balah, Gaza, and Jabalia (Ziv 2002).

One of the consequences of this infrastructure of checkpoints and blockades was the constitution of "enclaves" throughout the rural areas of the West Bank. These *enclaves* are rural areas to which all road accesses are closed, without any possibility of reaching medical centers in the nearby cities by any vehicle, even ambulances. Ambulances are unable to cross ditches of a depth of two to three meters or to climb embankments five meters high (Weingarten and Ziv 2003). A patient who has to be transferred to the hospital is brought by a vehicle to one side of the blockade and then transported by hand to an ambulance waiting for him/her at the other side.

Restrictions on movement have made access to more sophisticated health care facilities extremely difficult for those residing in the rural areas and smaller cities. Chronically ill patients and pregnant women are the principal groups affected by these restrictions. For example, dialysis patients, whose lives depend on regular hospital treatment, are subjected to innumerable bureaucratic requirements and delays. In times of siege, they do not receive treatment for several days (Ziv 2002).

Pregnant women have also had serious difficulties reaching a hospital. Hanan Zayyed, a pregnant woman expecting twins, is one of the many pregnant women delayed at a checkpoint. In 2002 she left her home in Nahalin at 5:45 a.m. to reach a hospital in Bethlehem because she felt contractions. The distance between Nahalin and Bethlehem is some eight kilometers, and in normal circumstances it should take no more than ten to fifteen minutes to arrive at the hospital. Hanan Zayyed's car, however, was delayed at an army checkpoint, where she gave birth to her children at 6:10 and 7:15. "Since the soldiers at the checkpoint still refused to enable Hanan and her family to cross, they were obliged to break through the checkpoint in order to reach the hospital. The delay proved fateful. Hanan Zayyed finally got to the hospital two hours after leaving home. Both her babies died shortly after arriving at hospital" (Ziv 2002, 17).

In theory, the Israel Defense Forces (IDF) orders stated that pregnant women close to delivery should be allowed to pass the checkpoints. But these orders are interpreted in different ways by commanders at the various checkpoints. Furthermore, soldiers at the checkpoints are not prepared to determine which women are close to delivery and which are not. In many cases they have simply refused to let pregnant women cross the checkpoints. Things are even worst when pregnant women arrive at unmanned blockades, which present often insurmountable obstacles.

Obstacles in access have affected the rate of hospital births, which have dropped more than 30 percent during the years following the outbreak of the first Intifadah. The increased rate of stillbirths mentioned above was not only the result of deteriorating socioeconomic conditions but also of difficulties in access to medical care. As mentioned before, systematization of hospital delivery in the fist two decades of the Occupation greatly contributed to the reduction in infant mortality rates and rise in life expectancy. The system of checkpoints and blockades compromised pregnant women's ability to deliver their babies in hospitals, and the rate of home deliveries and stillbirths increased as a result (Ziv et al. 2003).

While Israel holds de facto sovereignty in the OPT, its propaganda has emphasized Palestinian responsibility over services in general and health care in particular. The Occupation establishment has not taken responsibility for any problems experienced by chronically ill patients and pregnant women. Despite the many documented cases of pregnant women being delayed at the checkpoints or at unmanned blockades, Dalia Bessa, the health coordinator for the Civil Administration in the West Bank, claimed that this was a myth: "[T]he myth of the woman giving birth at the checkpoint is not always correct. The problem is that Palestinian women come to hospital at the last minute—not like us, where the woman rushes off to hospital every time she has a contraction. At Hadassah [hospital], they often give birth in the emergency room. The Palestinian ambulance drivers are very embarrassed, because the women give birth in the ambulance while it is on its way" (quoted in Ziv 2002, 18).

Bessa also insisted that it is an exaggeration to say that there are many unmet health care needs in the OPT. The proof of this falsehood, she said, could be seen in the lower hospitalization rates since the beginning of the second Intifadah. This argument ignores the fact that the decrease in hospitalization rates was not a function of decreasing health care problems but of restrictions on freedom of movement. Because of these restrictions, hospital facilities have operated at extremely low capacity for many years.[8]

The effect of restrictions on movement on access to emergency health care services was assessed by a 2006 study that showed that almost 20 percent of the patients treated in emergency rooms reported being delayed at checkpoints or having to make a detour to reach the hospital. Hospital admission was significantly more common for these patients (32% of delayed patients were admitted compared with 13% of patients who were not delayed). This fact suggests that blockades and checkpoints produce a deterioration in health and therefore increase costs, since hospital treatment is much more expensive than ambulatory treatment (Rytter et al. 2006).

As a consequence of the extended structure of checkpoints and blockades that divided the OPT into several cells, a complicated system of permits and authorizations was established in 1993. Permits are needed to pass the checkpoints and travel from one territorial cell to another. Entering Israel from the West Bank or the Gaza Strip is even more difficult. Palestinians living in the cities close to the Green Line,[9] such Tul Karem or Kalkilya, had to pass at least two checkpoints, but Palestinians living in more distant villages or towns might have to pass four or five checkpoints or unmanned obstacles. The first step to obtaining a permit is to get a magnetic card, which since 1989 is required to get a transit permit and then a working permit. The multiplication of internal checkpoints, which require transit permits, has turned the magnetic card into a lifesaving document for chronically ill patients.

Getting a permit card does not depend on the severity of the individual's medical condition but on the absence of a prohibition on alleged security or police grounds. Indeed, the restrictions on passage in the OPT are characterized by their arbitrary nature. This arbitrariness is not accidental. The opacity and randomness of the system constitutes a form of control no less effective than the restrictions on passage themselves (Filc 2004b). When nothing is transparent, when it is not clear who will receive a permit and who will not, when one official says that there is no restriction on passage but a second official does not give the permit, control becomes absolute.

If restrictions were consistent, then people would be able to plan their steps. They would know what to expect. There would be a possibility—albeit minimal—of choice. When decisions appear random, control becomes absolute. No one can be sure that he or she has not been—or will not be—"prohibited for reasons of security." The reasons for these prohibitions are so numerous, and the use made of them so variable, that uncertainty becomes the ultimate system of control within the framework of the certainty of the Occupation. Those opposed to the Occupation— demonstrators, journalists, some workers, direct victims of army or settler violence—are all potentially "prohibited for reasons of security." From this perspective, the permit is not a means of easing access for residents, but a way of controlling them through the threat of not giving a permit (Filc 2004b).

The arbitrariness of the permit system sometimes subjects Palestinians in the OPT to double jeopardy. If someone in the family is killed or injured by the IDF, this transforms the family into a security threat because Israeli officials claim that it is "more likely that they will be involved in a terrorist attack" (Ziv 2003, 16). The case of Muhammad Tabazeh tragically exemplifies this. On October 20, 2003, the Israeli air force shot two rockets at a car whose passengers were suspected of being Hamas activists in the Nusseirat refugee camp in the Gaza Strip. Many residents who arrived at the scene after the first rocket were hit by the second, including Mahmoud Tabazeh, a fourteen-year-old boy. Because of his serious condition, he was transferred for treatment to Tel Hashomer hospital. His brother Abed, aged twenty-three, a student of economics and statistics, was killed by the rocket, as was his cousin Ibrahim, a schoolboy in the twelfth grade who traveled with them. His father Muhammad had a permit to work in Israel, but after the attack his permit was canceled, and he was not allowed to visit his son, who was hospitalized in Israel. When he asked why, he was told, "it is because of your children, because of what happened to your family." Because his sons were injured by the IDF he was considered a "security threat," his permit was canceled, and his son Mahmoud had to undergo an extremely serious and complicated operation without a single member of his family at his bedside (Ziv 2003, 17).

Access to hospitals in Israel is not the only problem for Palestinians. Since the beginning of the second Intifadah, they also face many obstacles getting needed medicines within the OPT. The import of medicines into the Palestinian Authority via international borders is subject to the supervision and authorization of the Israeli authorities. This authorization is not always given in time, as in the case of Dr. Hassan Barghouti, a lecturer in literature at Al-Quds University. Barghouti suffered from cancer. Following the recommendation of his physician at Sheikh Zayed Hospital in

Ramallah, a hospital in Jordan sent him his needed medication. A special courier from the Jordanian hospital came to Allenby Crossing, the bridge that crosses the Jordan River and connects the West Bank and Jordan, with the medicine but was not permitted to cross to Ramallah. The Civil Administration held the drug, making its release dependent on answers to numerous questions. The authorities demanded to know whether the medicine was intended for one patient or more, whether it was donated or purchased, whether it was in a box or a bottle, what legend it bore, who sent it, and so on. The authorities then demanded medical documents proving that this specific medicine was indeed required for Barghouti, as well as the precise name of the medicine. The medical coordinator for the Civil Administration, Dalia Bessa, also demanded medical documents before approving passage of the medicine. Two days later Barghouti passed away. The same day a telephone call from the Civil Administration asked for yet another medical document in order to issue the permit for the passage of the medicine (Ziv 2002). While the drug would not have cured Barghouti's cancer, this story illustrates the way in which bureaucratic control over medicines and drugs functions as an instrument of the Occupation apparatus.

The construction of the "security fence/wall" within the West Bank—which was begun in 2002—has added yet another obstacle to Palestinians' access to health care. Until the construction of the wall, hospitals in East Jerusalem provided services for all the villages in the surroundings. A survey among inhabitants of those villages showed that almost 40 percent claimed that the fence/wall made their access to medical care more difficult (Kimhi and Hoshen 2006). The percentage of Palestinians in the villages around Jerusalem who received medical services in Jerusalem (mostly at East Jerusalem) decreased from 56 percent before the second Intifadah to 19 percent after 2004. Sixty-nine percent of the population in those villages used to receive services at Jerusalem hospitals before 2000. After 2004, the number decreased to 29 percent. Among the Palestinian inhabitants in Jerusalem, 30 percent reported that they had changed their health care provider because of the wall (Kimhi 2006).

Barta'a is one of those enclaves. Palestinian ambulances are not allowed to enter the enclave without special permission from the Jenin district coordination office (DCO).[10] Despite the existence of additional gates along the wall, ambulances can pass through only at the Barta'a checkpoint. Due to the requirement for special coordination of emergency transfer of patients, evacuation sometimes takes several hours or longer, delaying the transfer of patients who need immediate care to the hospital. Some patients thus prefer to get to Barta'a checkpoint on their own and to wait for an ambulance there. In both cases, though, there are significant delays that put those patients' health at risk (PHR 2004).

Blockades and checkpoints are not the only barrier to health care for Palestinians. Direct assaults on health care personnel and limitations on movement of health care providers have exacerbated the problems Palestinians face when they are sick. According to data from the Palestinian Red Crescent, "ambulances are able to reach the place where the sick or wounded are located only thirty percent of the time. In seventy percent of cases the sick or wounded must get to a location accessible to the ambulance on their own" (Swissa 2003, 7). In some cases even ambulances have been attacked. An example of this occurred in March 2002, when a Red Crescent ambulance carrying three crew members and a physician, Dr. Khalil Suleiman, set out for the Jenin refugee camp to try to evacuate people injured during the "Defensive Shield" operation. Even though the ambulance's trip was coordinated with the International Red Cross and the Israeli Civil Administration, the IDF opened fire on the ambulance, which then exploded. Dr. Suleiman was killed in the attack, and the other three crew members suffered serious burns.[11]

During the most violent periods of the conflict, hospitals have also been the target of harassment by the IDF. For example, on March 31, 2002, at 10 p.m., security forces accompanied by dogs undertook a search of the Arab Care center. The medical staff, physicians, and nurses were taken into one room and their hands tied behind their backs. A month later the Israeli security forces entered the Red Crescent maternity hospital in El-Bireh, gathered together all the workers and patients in the hospital, "including women who had given birth and new-born babies aged between 3 and 10 hours. The soldiers subsequently demanded that the director of the hospital, Dr. Auda Abu Nahla, and another staff member accompany them as they searched the hospital rooms. When unable to open doors, the soldiers broke them down with large metal bars" (Ziv 2003).

In sum, as a result of the economic crisis and the escalation in violence precipitated by the Occupation, the health care needs of the Palestinian population have grown while their access to health care and the ability of the system to meet the growing needs has sharply declined. In a 2002 study, following the escalation in the conflict in the early 2000s, respondents reported obstacles to curative services: 28.6 percent did not obtain medical care due to lack of drugs, 32.9 percent had no money, 26.6 percent could not reach a health center, and 16.8 percent reported that the health care personnel could not reach the health center (PCBS 2002). The increasing difficulty in reaching more complex health care facilities has overloaded the primary care system (WHO 2003).

Public health and preventive care have also been impaired. The rate of immunization—a key indicator for public health—has decreased, especially in remote areas. As a consequence of the decrease in the rate of hospital delivery, preventive measures such as hepatitis B vaccination and screening for phenylketonuria have severely decreased (Gordon and Filc 2007).

The disengagement from the Gaza Strip and Hamas's success in the Palestinian elections in 2005 marked another step in the escalation of violence. Prime Minister Ariel Sharon opted for unilateral disengagement from the Gaza Strip to avoid the renewal of peace talks that would follow the pattern of the Geneva initiative, signed by Palestinian and Israeli political figures, or the Arab League's initiative. The Geneva initiative was a joint proposition put forward by Israeli and Palestinian politicians and public figures that defined the grounds for a peace treatment. The Arab League's initiative was a declaration by the Arab countries defining the grounds for global peace in the Middle East. Both initiatives included Israel's retreat to the pre–June 1967 borders, Jerusalem as the capital of Israel and the Palestinian state, and a negotiated solution to the refugees' issue. The unilateral disengagement was meant to avoid international pressure on Israel while, within Israel, strengthening the belief that there was no Palestinian partner for peace negotiations. For the first time since the Occupation, Israel dismantled Jewish settlements in the OPT, which could have been a catalyst for a new, more positive, dynamic in the conflict. However, the opportunity was missed due to Israel's ongoing repression and expansion of settlements in the West Bank (as if the West Bank and the Gaza Strip were two different political entities), and Hamas's hard-line approach, which denied any possible future recognition of Israel, even if Israel agreed to retreat to the Green Line and dismantle all the settlements. The IDF continued to chase Palestinians in the West Bank, and Hamas and the Islamic Jihad retaliated from the Gaza Strip.[12]

After Hamas's success in the Palestinian elections, an economic embargo was forced on the Hamas government. The embargo, which was supposed to pressure Hamas to soften its position, had the opposite effect. To retain public support for its government in the light of the ongoing hardships, Hamas choose a more violent path. This provoked an escalation of violence that reached its peak with Hamas's attack on the border and the abduction of soldier Guilad Shalit. Israel's violent retaliation caused tens of deaths and the destruction of vital infrastructure such as electricity generators. Finally Hamas's coup against Fatah further increased the death toll.[13] Israel has intentionally destroyed civilian infrastructures; for example, by bombing electric turbines. In Israel, the public seems indifferent to the fact that essential civil systems, such as the health care system,[14] can no longer function. All this has dealt a fatal blow to the Palestinian economy, resulting in severe poverty and in acute and chronic malnutrition and suggests an escalation in Israel's disposition to use increasing violence as a way of managing the conflict over the long run.

When Israel disengaged from the Gaza Strip, most of the Israeli public and government mistakenly concluded that the country could end its costly Occupation while still maintaining control over Gaza. In the government's view Israel would still be in control of all the entrances to Gaza and could use this control as a way of punishing and putting pressure on the Palestinians. The military operations within the West Bank continued, and settlements in the West Bank still expanded. The Israeli official position was that since the disengagement, Israel has no more responsibilities concerning the population of the Gaza strip.

The Palestinians in Gaza are seen as a collective hostage in the conflict between Israel and Hamas. Thus, the checkpoints can be closed (and this happens frequently[15]), leaving hundreds of patients who cannot receive therapy in the Gaza Strip (patients suffering from cancer, severe burns, and severe trauma) trapped in the area with no access to treatment. The politics of permits to the Gaza population has been hardened. It is much more difficult for Palestinians who live in the Gaza Strip to get a permit to enter Israel in 2008 than it was two years ago. There are more delays in answering requests and more patients who are refused for security reasons. Among the latter, only patients suffering from life-threatening conditions can apply to receive permits. Even then, on many occasions permits are denied for people suffering from severe, even terminal disease; and the Israeli security forces try to use permits as a way to obtain collaboration or to put pressure on the Hamas leadership.[16] In many cases, such as that of a sixteen-year-old girl in urgent need of a cardiac valve replacement or a twenty-two-year-old woman suffering from Hodgkin's lymphoma, permits require a long process of discussions, pressure, and intervention from Israeli human rights NGOs before being approved. Unfortunately, there were also patients in risk of death or loosing a limb whose petitions were denied and where no pressure helped.

In the previous chapters I have analyzed the ways in which violations to the right to health and exclusion from health care services take place within Israel. This chapter shows that the violations to the right to health, lack of the social determinants of health, and obstacles in access to health care services are much worse in the OPT. Since the 1993 Oslo agreements, Israel adamantly claims that the Palestinian Authority is responsible for governing the Palestinians in the OPT. Israel says the PA is responsible for all that happens in the OPT, including health services. As we have seen, however, Israel is the de facto sovereign in the OPT, utilizing military force as well as controlling access and roads. Israel severs the link between the two terms of the classical formulation of sovereignty by Thomas Hobbes: *protego ergo obligo* (protection therefore obedience), or since I confer protection I can demand obedience (Hobbes 1958). Israel exercises power over the Palestinians in the OPT but transfers responsibility for protection (providing the basic resources, health care, education, and so on) to the Palestinian Authority, thus freeing itself of the responsibility that results from the prolonged Occupation. Thus, insofar as a just peace agreement does not put an end to the Occupation following the lines of the Geneva agreement and the Arab League initiative, Israel must be held responsible for the health status and access to health care of the Palestinians in the OPT.

CONCLUSION

In the National Health Insurance (NHI) law passed in 1994, the Israeli government formally based its health care system on the values of
justice, equality, and mutual help. The third article of the law definitively
stated that every resident is entitled to health care services and that access
to health treatment will depend on medical considerations and will be of
reasonable quality. These two articles could provide the legal basis for the
recognition of equal access to health care, as a social right. Indeed, in many
ways they do. The law established an institutional framework that provided coverage for all Israeli residents that is recognized by the Ministry of
Internal Affairs. It detached the quality and quantity of services from the
ability to pay for them. It provided an institutional way to express the solidarity between the elderly and the young (since the former paid less and
received more, and the latter financed the difference). It built a "single-
payer" system in which four public, nonprofit sick funds are responsible
for the provision of services.

This structure has the benefits of both a public system and a very limited form of managed competition. The public system is nonprofit, ensures equality of access, and gives the state responsibility for the financing of health care and ensuring social solidarity. Utilizing a highly restricted form of managed competition allows the system to be somewhat competitive. The four sick funds must provide good services to attract members, but prices and the scope of services are the same for all the sick funds and are established by law.

In 1995, at the time the law was implemented, 75 percent of the national health expenditure was publicly financed, and 25 percent was privately financed. This distribution was slightly worse than that of the more egalitarian European countries, where the balance between public and private sources was closer to 80 percent public, 20 percent private. This is largely because in Israel, dentistry (which represents some 10 percent of the national health expenditure) is not covered by the public system. While a more egalitarian health care system should also include dentistry, the NHI law did provide for a relatively egalitarian, mostly public, health care system—the approach favored by most Israelis who see the state as responsible for the provision of health care.

Like many European health care systems, the Israeli health care system is very different from the U.S. health care model where the state is not responsible for the provision of health care to its citizens and where health care seems to be viewed as a source of profit for the insurance industry, the pharmaceutical companies, and the medical establishment.

As we have seen in the previous chapters, the positive characteristics of the NHI law notwithstanding, the Israeli health care system is far from equal and is moving in an increasingly "Americanized" direction. Access to health care in Israel is characterized by circles of exclusion. Those circles are delimited by three main axes: (1) the Occupation, (2) the institutional structure of citizenship, and (3) the neoliberalization of Israeli society and the health care field.

The Occupation, as we have seen, affects not only access to health care but the health status of the Palestinians in the OPT. Occupation negatively affects the health of Palestinians not only through direct violence but also through its deleterious influence on the social determinants of health in the OPT. As the violence of the Occupation has increased, especially after the beginning of the second Intifadah, the quality of daily life in the OPT has worsened. Poverty, malnutrition, limitations on freedom of movement, severe restrictions in access to services in Israel that cannot be found in the OPT—these are only some of the myriad ways in which the Occupation damages the health of Palestinians, limits their access to health care, and impacts their rights as human beings.

In Israel, the institutional structure of citizenship—understood as a set of practices and institutions that "shape the flow of resources to persons and social groups" (Turner 1993, 2)—also makes it difficult for Israeli Palestinians, migrant workers, and asylum seekers to get needed health care services. As we have seen, due to geographic segregation and institutional—not legal—discrimination in ability to acquire land and find resources for investment, health indicators (e.g., mortality and life expectancy) for Israeli Palestinians are worse than those of Israeli Jews. While Israeli Palestinians are covered by the NHI law, when they try to obtain the services that are easily accessible to Jewish Israelis, they must navigate a maze of obstacles that are a direct result of the underdevelopment of services in their towns and villages. Obstacles such as language and different conceptions about health and disease exacerbate an already untenable situation.

As we saw in chapter 3, the unequal structure of citizenship also plays a major role in not only creating inequalities but also seriously jeopardizing the health status of the Bedouins in the unrecognized villages in the Negev region. There is simply no way for people to maintain their health or care for themselves or their loved ones when they are sick if they lack clean water, sewage, and electricity. Finally, in the case of migrant workers and asylum seekers, the characteristics of citizenship in Israel make the blatant exclusion of migrant workers legal because, under the NHI law, access to health care is dependent on being an officially recognized resident.

This exclusion is certainly not inevitable. Including migrant workers under the public health care system, as do countries such as Spain and Holland, makes sense from both a human rights and public health perspective. Moreover, from the perspective of welfare economics, providing good primary care is always more cost-effective than treating life-threatening complications. However, the strength of the discriminatory character of citizenship in Israel precludes any consideration of the obvious advantages of including migrant workers and asylum seekers into the public health care system.

Finally, the third axis of exclusion is the neoliberalization/Americanization of Israeli society and of the health care field. Israel's economy has grown significantly in the last two decades. Israel's per capita GDP today is higher than the per capita GDP of countries such as Spain, Italy, and even France (IMF 2007). However, the rapid growth has been unequally distributed. Today Israel has one of the biggest socioeconomic gaps of the rich countries of the world (second only to the United States). As epidemiologists such as Richard Wilkinson and Ichiro Kawachi have shown, unequal societies are unhealthy societies (Wilkinson 1996; Kawachi and Kennedy 2006). Thus it is hardly surprising that the unequal distribution of wealth influences the health status of Israelis—not just Israeli Palestinians but poorer and older Israeli Jews as well.

The advent of increasing privatization of Israeli health care has undermined the ability of the NHI law to fulfill its promise. While the law still provides the legal framework for a mostly public health care system and guarantees state responsibility for the provision of health care, decisions like the abolition of the earmarked employers' tax or the introduction of copayments have significantly eroded the scope and goals of the law. As the financing of the national expenditure in health care shifts from the public purse to the private pocket (today the rate is 68% public, 32% private), the poorest 20 percent of the Israeli population no longer get all the high-quality services that the Israeli health care system can provide.

The three axes that build the circles of exclusion are not independent of one another but interact to produce and reproduce exclusion. The prolonged conflict and the militarization of Israeli society facilitated the emergence of an economy based on the security industries and—since the mid-1980s—the security-related high-tech industry. Forty years of Occupation have paved the way for the consolidation of a dual labor market characterized by a high-income sector linked to the high-tech sector and high-skilled services and a low-income sector consisting of unskilled services, residual labor-intensive industry, construction, and agriculture. This dual market economy requires low-wage workers. When the escalation of the Israeli-Palestinian conflict limited the scope of work of Palestinians from the OPT, migrant laborers from other countries replaced them. Moreover, as we saw in chapter 5, the costs of the Occupation and the prolonged conflict influence the need to limit social expenditure; this, in turn, limits the resources available for the health care system.

The structure of citizenship and the neoliberalization process also interact, for neoliberalism has a particularly hard impact on groups of lower socioeconomic status. Due to both segregation and discrimination, Israeli

Palestinians are thus overrepresented among the lower socioeconomic sectors. They find it difficult to insert themselves in the high-wage sectors and suffer from the cuts in welfare expenditure. In Israel, poll after poll has documented that Israeli Jewish citizens strongly support both the public health care system and the concept of publicly funded education and health care. Brookdale Institute surveys, done after the implementation of the NHI law, document that over 80 percent of Israelis report personal satisfaction with the services their health care system provides them. Satisfaction was greater among Israeli Arabs, probably reflecting the equalizing effect of the law and the fact that almost 25 percent of them, who before 1995 lacked health insurance, now had much better access to health care services. Other surveys suggest that more than 60 percent of Israelis do not favor privatization. Despite this fact, the continued concern for security that stems from the Occupation and conflict with Palestinians makes it very difficult to create a political movement that would harness both public support for public health care and disaffection with privatization.

Many poorer and elderly Jews—whether in the periphery or Mizrahim—who have suffered because of eroding health care services could join with progressive middle-class Jews and Palestinian Israelis to form a movement that would effectively challenge those who promote the notion that health care should be a commodity provided for and regulated by the not-so-invisible hand of the market. Many of these Israeli Jews are dissatisfied with the policies of leaders such as Benjamin Netanyahu—prime minister from June 1996 to July 1999 and leader of the conservative Likud party—who was repudiated in the polls for his attacks on public services in Israel. But each time a bomb or rocket explodes in Israel, the concern for security overrides issues—like the state of the health care system—that affects Israelis on a daily basis as much as or even more than does the Arab-Israeli conflict. Similarly, although Israeli Palestinians have a clear interest in aligning with Israeli Jews around health care issues, the longtime exclusion and discrimination have created a feeling of otherness or foreignness that is difficult to overcome. As long as the conflict continues, the political and party system will focus on conflict-related issues that make it difficult to articulate the fact that a majority of both Israeli Jews and Palestinians oppose privatization. This, in turn, thwarts the creation of an organized political opposition.

As a consequence of these three distinct but interrelated axes of exclusion, the positive characteristics of the NHI law do not result in a truly inclusive and egalitarian health care system. Instead they create a set of ever-widening circles of exclusion that produce differential access to health care and reproduce and reinforce the exclusionary characteristics of Israeli society. The circles of exclusion that I have described are unacceptable not only because of the negative impact they have on the health of those caught behind their borders but also because exclusion is a dynamic, not a static, process. Once the process of exclusion is seen to be legitimate, the mentality of Occupation and denial does not stop at the Green Line. Many young Israelis have become convinced that it is acceptable for them to enjoy greater health care access and better services than Bedouins or migrant workers or Palestinians in the OPT. They do not protest a system in which the sick funds sell complementary insurance that provides services that are not accessible for all—even to their parents or grandparents. This erosion of a sense of solidarity threatens the health of more and more Israelis.

The picture I have painted is critical of the current structure and tendencies of Israeli state and society. In Israel today, there is a robust debate about the issues raised in this book. When this critique crosses the Atlantic, however, it becomes far more politically and emotionally charged than it is inside Israel itself. As I address an American audience, I am thus conscious that many may regard this critique as being anti-Israel and that some will even accuse me of being "anti-Semitic" or of providing support for those who would deny the legitimacy of the very existence of Israel. I think that it would be sadly ironic if those who have not consciously and deliberately chosen to live in Israel make this allegation against someone who has.

I am convinced that it is important to be critical of the ways in which Israel builds circles of exclusion that affect access to health care. To those who would silence such critical voices I would like to answer by quoting a few lines from a poem by the Polish poet and 1996 Nobel Prize winner Wislawa Szymborska, entitled "In Praise of Feeling Bad About Yourself."

> The buzzard never says it is to blame.
> The panther wouldn't know what scruples mean.
> When the piranha strikes, it feels no shame....
> On this third planet of the sun
> among the signs of bestiality
> a clear conscience is Number One. (Szymborska 2000, 168)

This book is written from a profound identification with Israeli society. I wrote this book motivated by the conviction that pointing to Israeli society's

defects while working to modify them is the true and only way of supporting the existence of Israel. As I argued in the Introduction, pointing out to
someone very dear to you that his or her lifestyle is damaging to his or her
health is a moral obligation. The obligation stems from the depth of one's
caring and concern.

If we move from the patient or family member to the state, I am also
convinced that ignoring Israel's problems—taking an Israel right or wrong
position—endangers the very state whose existence we are trying to protect. The Occupation is not only morally wrong, but it is the main obstacle
for a peaceful resolution of the conflict, and it endangers us all. Israel's future depends on its—our—ability to resolve problems and maintain social
solidarity. To continue on the path that we are on is self-destructive. We,
Israeli and Palestinians, simply cannot continue to pay the costs of continuous conflict and of the denial of basic rights to so many who live either in
Israel or, especially so, in the Occupied Territories.

There are solutions to all the problems described in this book. The
circles of exclusion I have explored are not God-given or "natural" phe-
nomena; they are man-made. Their abolition is not a dream, an impossible
utopia such as the Jewish messianic realm, the Christian millennium, or the
Marxian "kingdom of freedom." While today solutions may seem utopian,
they are, in fact, "realistic utopias" if we adopt a "right to health" perspective. As we saw in the Introduction, a universal and egalitarian conception
of the right to health provides a framework that transcends the specificity of
the Israeli situation or of the Israeli-Palestinian conflict. The idea of the
right to health as universal and equal—including not only equal access
and equal quality for equal need but also the social conditions necessary to
maximize everybody's chances to enjoy good health—is a claim based on
the awareness of our vulnerability as human beings.

The claim to a universal and egalitarian right to health has different
concrete expressions in different societies. In the United States, for example, one of its main expressions is the claim to universal access to health
care services for American citizens lacking insurance; in Europe, the inclusion of migrant workers excluded from the health care system.

In the Israeli context, a universal right to health means breaking the
circles of exclusion that structure access to services and resources. Breaking
the circles of exclusion means first and foremost the end of the Occupation and the establishment of a Palestinian state in accord with the lines

of the Arab League or the Geneva Agreement and, in the future, maybe even a confederation including both Palestine and Israel. It means, after the prolonged Occupation, assuming Israel's responsibility toward Palestinian society.

It is possible to end Israel's Occupation and begin the process of the establishment of a Palestinian state as envisioned by the Arab League and the Geneva initiatives. Ending the Occupation would also be a crucial first step toward building a different relationship with Israeli Palestinians. However, a new kind of relationship requires eliminating the structural discrimination and exclusion of Israeli Palestinians, guaranteeing their equal access to land, modifying the criteria for distribution of material resources at the various levels of state activity, redistributing resources to compensate for past discrimination, achieving agreements that ensure their right to cultural autonomy, and modifying the structure of citizenship.

In the field of health care this means viewing the elimination of the gap in health indicators between Jews and Israeli Palestinians as a national goal; bringing services in Arab cities, towns, and villages up to the level of those in the Jewish settlements; and building culturally sensitive services. It means recognizing the Bedouin villages in the Negev and supplying these towns with electricity, water, and sewage. It means constructing roads leading to the villages, opening medical clinics in all of them, and designing culturally sensitive health care services.

Breaking the circles of exclusion implies enlarging the scope of *jus solis* (i.e., legal notion that citizenship is determined by place of birth and not by the citizenship of one's parents) as a gate to citizenship so that every child born in Israel will be entitled to citizenship.[1] It requires the implementation of ways of naturalization for non-Jews, for all those for whom Israel has become home.

Moreover, as human rights organizations argue, visas for workers should be granted for longer periods, and migrant workers already living in Israel should be given priority in applying for jobs to put an end to the "revolving doors" policy. To end the exploitation linked to brokerage and binding, the visa must be given directly to the worker rather than to the employer or manpower company.

Breaking the circles of exclusion also requires giving all migrants residing and working in Israel who are not interested in naturalization the possibility of "social citizenship."

Migrant workers should be guaranteed all civic and social rights even though they do not have political rights (either because they are yet citizens or because they are not interested in staying in Israel in the long run). As the Hotline for Migrant Workers, a Israeli human rights organization, put it on its homepage, "A person 'good enough' to be part of the Israeli economy is 'good enough' to be part of the Israeli society."

Migrant workers and their children should be incorporated into the NHI program. Documented migrant workers can pay the health tax as a percentage of their wages, as do Israeli citizens. A special program could also be created that would allow undocumented workers to pay a minimum tax even though they are not officially registered as workers. Asylum seekers should also be included under the NHI program until they will be officially recognized as refugees.

Social citizenship would be the first step in the process of integration of migrant workers into Israeli society. Zeev Rosenhek has explained why this is so important: "[S]ince the welfare state domain is one of the most important sites at which membership in the polity is constituted and actualized, the extension of social rights tends not only to contribute to an improvement in their living conditions and life chances, but also to have broad effects on their political status" (Rosenhek 2007, 227).

The first changes that may point to attempts to break the circles of exclusion have occurred in the arena of social citizenship. As discussed in chapter 4, in 2006 the Israeli government gave a few hundred children of migrant workers the right to legal residence and eventual access to citizenship. As Rosenhek argues, this act, although still a one-time event, represents a breakthrough in the Israeli context. In Rosenhek's words, "[T]he recognition of labor migrants' children as potential members of society was justified on the grounds that they 'have assimilated into Israeli society and culture' and their deportation 'would be akin to cultural exile to a country which [they have] no cultural ties.' This formulation signals a significant departure from the dominant ethnic-Jewish understanding of Israeli nationhood and culture" (Rosenhek 2007, 228). This could mark the beginning of migrant workers' inclusion.

Finally, breaking the circles of exclusion means reversing the process of neoliberalization and Americanization of Israeli society, especially concerning the privatization of welfare and in particular of the health care system. In the field of health care, the NHI law provides an excellent legal basis for the consolidation of a universal and egalitarian health care system; while the existence of four nonprofit, public sick funds and an excellent network of public hospitals provide the institutional basis for a just health care system. This basis should be improved, however, through inclusive policies in the field of mental health, the expansion of prevention, the abolition of economic obstacles (such as copayments) to access health care, and the actualization of the "basket" of services provided by the public sector.

I echo many others in proposing these solutions as a way to make Israeli society more just, inclusive, and humane. Exposing and analyzing the forms of injustice, inequality, and inhumanity that take place in my country and my society has not been easy. In this sense this is a book written with pain, and also with shame. But this book is also written with hope, for I am convinced that the circles of exclusion can be broken. Hope is based on the several organizations and movements in Israel that support and struggle for some, or all, of these changes: human rights organizations, patients' organizations, peace movements. We should not, however, confuse hope with easy optimism because most of these proposals do not find enough support within the party system and state institutions. To break the circles of exclusion, support for the changes mentioned above should expand from civil society to the political system. This is a long and difficult process but one that is possible and worth the struggle.

NOTES

Introduction: Four Stories of Exclusion

1. All patients' names in the book are pseudonyms.

2. The Israeli sick funds are organizations that, like the U.S. health maintenance organizations (HMOs), are both insurers and providers of health care services. In Israel there are four sick funds. Kupat Holim Clalit, or Clalit Sick Fund, was the sick fund of the workers' union, and due to tradition and ideology it was the only fund that provided services for the poorest sectors. As will be explained in greater detail in chapter 3, in the 1980s and early 1990s its financial situation was dire, and its per capita expenditure was significantly less than the other sick funds.

3. By "Americanization" I mean the adoption of institutional patterns and social culture based on, among other features, individualism, consumerism, and opposition to state provision of welfare services.

4. Child allowances are a transfer payment paid by the state to every family for every child under eighteen.

5. The Oslo agreements between Israel and the PLO were the beginning of a peace process that was supposed to end in Israel's retreat from the Occupied Territories, the establishment of a Palestinian state, and the recognition of Israel by the Palestinians.

1. The Israeli Health Care System: An Overview

1. The passage of the National Health Insurance (NHI) act marks a seminal change, so much so that it can be considered as the beginning of a new period, but such change is inscribed in a more general tendency toward the commodification of health care.

2. Mapai, acronym for Mifleget Poalei Eretz Israel (Party of the Workers of the Land of Israel), was the main party within the Yshuv and was the dominant Israeli party until 1977.

3. The Progressive era refers to the period between 1890 and 1920 in the United States. *Progressivism* is a term to characterize a range of economic, political, social, and moral reforms promoted by sectors among the white, educated, and well-off elite. These reforms included efforts to outlaw the sale of alcohol, to regulate child labor and sweatshops, to restrict immigration and "Americanize" immigrants, and to regulate trusts. Within the health field, progressives emphasized public health and sought to address health hazards through education and hygiene measures. They also tried, and failed, to pass legislation that would ensure government provision of health insurance.

4. Jewish immigrants arrived in Israel in several waves. The second one (1904–1914) included Polish and Russian Jews, most of them identified with one of the various socialist currents.

5. Most patients in government hospitals were Muslim Arabs (85% in 1944), and these hospitals' staff was usually Arab.

6. The two parties—Ahdut Ha'avoda and Hapoel Hatzair—would merge in 1930 to form the party of the Workers of the Land of Israel: Mapai.

7. Thus, until the establishment of the state in 1948, there were no Arab members of the Histadrut.

8. The Revisionist Zionist party, a right-wing party, broke with the Zionist Federation, and its members and institutions became almost anathema in the discourse of the Yishuv's leadership.

9. Middle-class and national religious sectors were subaltern members of the historical bloc.

10. The Austrian social democratic party supported a "third way" between communism and reformist social democracy. One of the elements of this third way was the development of working class autonomous institutions—such as sick funds, schools, and adult education.

11. Halevy quotes Mapai's Finance Minister Pinhas Sapir as saying that "every pound which I invest in Kupat Holim [the Histadrut's sick fund] is worth more to me than the same pound which I invest in the Ministry of Health" (Halevy 1980, 91).

12. The ineffectiveness of the MOH resulted from the fact that, until 1977, the Minister of Health was usually a member of one of the weakest parties in the governing coalition.

13. Even though the National Health Insurance (NHI) act prescribes that the provision of mental health services should be transferred to the sick funds, these services are still provided by the MOH.

14. The health tax is an earmarked mandatory tax paid by every worker and senior citizen, amounting to 4.8% of wages.

15. As we will see in chapter 2, the Knesset rejected a Ministry of Finance initiative to allow for-profit sick funds.

16. Copayment at this level is highly ineffective because preventive services are the most cost-effective, and access should be encouraged and not limited by copayments.

17. Pregnancy- and delivery-related mortality do not explain the small gap in life expectancy between men and women, since the maternal mortality rate in Israel is one of the lowest in the world, at 3 deaths per 100,000 live births during the 1980–92 period.

18. The same year Denmark spent 6.7% of its GDP on health, the United Kingdom 7.1%, the Netherlands 8.7%, Canada 10.2%, and the United States 14.1%.

19. CBS data does not distinguish between paramedical jobs (such as laboratory or radiology technicians and occupational and speech therapists), administrative and managerial jobs, and maintenance jobs.

20. Until 1996, there was a parallel tax paid by employers to the National Insurance Institute and distributed among the sick funds by the same capitation formula. This tax was abolished in 1997 as a concession to employers.

21. As household participation in financing grows, inequality in access and quality of care grows as well. In 1992/1993 (the latest figures available), Jewish households spent some NIS 370 a month on health, whereas Arab households spent 24% less. A similar gap was found between the health expenditures of Ashkenazi and Mizrahi Jews (450 and 327 respectively), even if some of the differences may be due to age disparities (CBS 1993; B. Swirski et al. 1998).

22. This does not characterize solely the Israeli case. Discussing T. H. Marshall's theory of the development of citizens' rights in Great Britain, B. Hindess claims that "beneath Marshall's account of the status of citizenship and the rights and duties, it is not difficult to discern the model of the community as a democratic republic that Western political thought has inherited from the civic republicanism of early modern Europe" (Hindess 1993, 26–27).

23. There are limits to freedom of expression and association, however; associations and publications that challenge the definition of Israel as a Jewish state may be banned.

24. In 1993, the country with the lowest infant mortality rate was Finland, with 4.4 deaths per 1,000 live births. The highest rate among OECD countries is the United State's—8.5.

25. In 1993, Japan had the highest life-expectancy rate for both men and women—76.0 and 82.2 respectively. Sweden's life expectancy for the same year was 80.6 for women and 75.4 for men; the United State's life expectancy was 79.1 for women and 72.4 for men. Life expectancy in Israel in 1993 was 78.4 for women and 74.6 for men.

26. Migrant workers, whether "legal" or "illegal," are not included in the law.

27. For example, more health care workers in all fields (with the exception of family doctors) reside in the big cities and in the central district than in the North or the South. Dentists are concentrated in the three largest cities in the center area, where 90% of them practice (Shuval 1992).

28. Note that the NHI act has had two important positive effects on health care for Arab citizens. First, until this law was passed, 25% of Arab citizens did not have health insurance. Since then, all of them have the right to the national health basket. Second, competition among the sick funds has led to the establishment of more ambulatory services in Arab communities, resulting in greater accessibility and quality improvement (B. Swirksi et al. 1998).

2. The "Neoliberalization" of the Israeli Health Care System

1. Stanley Fisher has been president of Israel's Central Bank since 2005.

2. Throughout the 2000s, Israel has been the largest recipient of U.S. military aid in the world, before Egypt and Colombia (vaughns-1-pagers.com/politics/us-foreign-aid.htm).

3. Milton Friedman was a professor of Economics at Chicago University and one of the central ideologists of economic neoliberalism.

4. The case-mix indicates the percentage of insured population suffering from chronic or diseases that require expensive treatments. Age-mix means the age distribution of the insured population, since age is the most important single variable that influences health expenditure.

5. The second component of private expenditure—private insurance—also expanded since the mid 1990s, even though it is still a relatively insignificant part of national health expenditure. Household spending on private insurance for dental care, emergency and acute medicine, and nursing care grew by 233% from 1986/87 to 1992/93, and the data show a steady increase in the number of health insurance policies between 1990 and 1994. A survey undertaken by the Gertner Institute between October 1993 and February 1994 showed that 18% of respondents had some sort of private health insurance (for dental care, emergencies, acute treatment, and nursing care), while 7% of the population had complementary insurance for acute or chronic treatments (Shmueli 2000). The demographic analysis of health insurance buyers also shows that commodification processes enhance inequality. Those who have private health insurance are younger, healthier, and richer than the average population, and more men than women buy private insurance.

6. State investigation committees in Israel have been used to investigate issues that are considered severe institutional failures, such as the 1973 Yom Kippur War, the assassination of Prime Minister Rabin, and the assassination of Muslims while praying by Baruch Goldstein. It should be noted that the Likud government also had a political interest in investigating the crisis because it wanted to weaken the KHC and the Histadrut, which were dominated by the Labor party.

7. The decay in the prestige of the Workers Central Union, the Histadrut (owner of KHC), was also a key issue in the young families' decision to leave KHC.

8. In Rosen et al's study, 4% of all those interviewed wanted to move to another sick fund but were rejected, while another 8% did not even try to transfer—despite their wish to do so—because they thought they would be rejected. Of all those rejected by a sick fund, 75% had applied to Maccabi (B. Rosen et al. 1995) and had been denied entry, mostly because of their age and health status. Maccabi did not enroll members over sixty and required potential members to undergo a medical examination, the results of which could be used to bar enrollment. All sick funds restricted the admission of chronically ill applicants (Chinitz 1995).

9. In 2002, for example, there was still a difference in membership income between the four sick funds. If we consider the mean income as 100, the mean membership income was 84.4 at Leumit, 93.6 at KHC, 107.8 at Meuhedet, and 118.6 at Maccabi.

10. Popular opposition expressed itself in demonstrations backed by physicians, nurses, and organizations of users of the health care service.

11. Between 1993 and 2000 the number of public beds increased another 16%, compared with 35% for private beds (CBS 2001).

12. In the last section I presented the figures from the point of view of health expenditure; in this section I will look at this process from the point of view of the health insurance industry.

13. It is difficult to compare the growth of the private sector until 2003 with its growth in the four years after 2003 because the Central Bureau of Statistics changed its definition of private and public. Since state-owned hospitals sell many services at market values, the CBS considers them now as part of the business sector, and not as part of the public sector. Thus the figures of the private sector's share for 2004 and 2005 were 47% and 48%.

14. Not all the costs are included in the primary clinics' budget. The budget, nowadays, includes all the purchased services and pharmaceuticals but excludes administrative costs and wages.

15. The users of the health care system do not always identify with this form of understanding the medical encounter. The patients who took part in the KHC think tank, for example, opposed the use of the term "client" to denominate users of health care services.

16. From now on, CHS (Clalit Health Services).

17. Hospitals competed for "attractive" physicians. In at least one case, KHC used a personal contract to offer sufficient financial compensation to a prominent cardiac surgeon who would otherwise have engaged in extensive private practice (Chinitz and Rosen 1991, 41).

18. The Sharan was developed with the blessing—if not the encouragement—of the MOH, which was more concerned with opening new fields for hospital revenues than with controlling total health expenditures as a percentage of the GDP.

3. The Health of Israeli Palestinians and Bedouins

1. In 2006 representatives from the Ministry of Internal Affairs planned to demolish several houses in Zahra's village, including hers. Following the intervention of a number of members of the Knesset, this decision was postponed but not canceled.

2. In 2006, infant mortality among Israeli Jews was 3.1/1,000 while among Israeli Arabs it was 7.7/1,000.

3. The figures are 1 for every 15.5 inhabitants, and 1 for 29.5 inhabitants accordingly.

4. The figures are NIS 241 for Jews and NIS 95 for Arabs.

5. The figures are NIS 387 per Jewish hospitalized patient vs. NIS 223 per Palestinian hospitalized patient.

6. Among the users of services, Jews have NIS 238 lower cost on average than do Arabs. The reason is that the propensity to use ambulatory—and cheaper—services is much higher among the Jews (Shmueli, 2000).

7. Prior to the legislation of the NHI law, lack of health insurance represented an additional barrier for Israeli Palestinians since a quarter of them lacked insurance.

8. Only an estimated 5% of Bedouins maintains a nomadic lifestyle, seasonally returning to a permanent residence (Pessate-Schubert 2003; Lewando-Hundt et al. 2001).

9. All of these indicators may be assumed to be lower for the unrecognized villages' population as compared with the state-planned settlements.

10. In Bedouin society, consanguinity and polygamy are common. A 2003 study found 60% of Bedouin women married to a cousin or other relative; 35% of women were in a polygamous marriage (Cwikel and Barak 2003).

11. Shalev et al. found that 13.8% of children with undifferentated febrile illness were positive for murine typhus (Shalev et al. 2006).

12. Filed on behalf of the residents of Unrecognized Villages and several organizations through the Association of Civil Rights in Israel and Adalah, the Legal Center for the Rights of the Arab Minority in Israel.

13. The recommended ratio is 1 physician per 1,200–1,400 residents.

14. Throughout the past decade, geographic barriers to care have been reduced by the establishment of clinics in some of the unrecognized villages and by the use of mobile immunization teams and a mobile MCH clinic.

15. If a private vehicle is used, the husband is usually behind the wheel.

4. Migrant Workers

1. Hamas, acronym for Harakat al-Muqawama al-Islamiyya or "Islamic Resistance Movement," is an Islamic fundamentalist Palestinian military and political organization, which since 2005 became the biggest party in the OPT.

2. Since there is no way to know the exact number of undocumented migrants, the figures are estimates by the Central Bureau of Statistics (CBS).

3. Sarah Willen describes a series of practices performed by the state, by employers or by the manpower firms, that result in the "illegalization" of migrant workers, including the confiscation of passports by the employer and the artificial inflation of demand for workers.

4. An *immigration regime* has been defined as the complex network of goals, agents, principles, institutions, and procedures by which the state manages immigration (Freeman 1992).

5. See chapter 2.

6. Currently, with few exceptions, non-Jewish immigrants may receive the benefits of citizenship only if they marry Israeli citizens (and even this is limited for Palestinian citizens).

7. Data from the CBS show that in most years, the number of documented migrant workers that arrived to Israel was higher than those who voluntarily left or were deported, meaning that the "revolving door" policy perpetuates the status of undocumented migrant workers.

8. Since 2003 this unit is part of the Ministry for Industry and Commerce.

9. There is a regulation that allows a migrant worker to change employers in certain special cases, such as a caregiver whose employer passed away.

10. Shas is an ultra-orthodox Mizrahi (Oriental Jews) party.

11. One of the rationales for the current agreement was to guarantee that migrant workers leave Israel after a certain period; the manpower companies would keep part of the workers' wages until the moment they left Israel, thus creating an economic incentive not to stay in Israel.

12. This is also the opinion of the Bank of Israel, which in its 2005 annual report stated: "[T] his agreement allows for binding the migrant worker to the manpower company and allows only for limited freedom. Moreover, the agreement creates a new middleman, increasing the cost of employment without increasing the workers' wages" (Bank of Israel 2005,182).

13. See chapters 2 and 3.

14. Rules for Migrant Workers-Fair Employment, 2000.

15. An arteriovenous fistula is an artificial connection between artery and vein, inserted for example for hemodialysis.

16. The experience of organizations that support migrant workers, such as the Hotline, the law clinic at Tel Aviv University, and Physicians for Human Rights is that when employers support the workers the latter have more leverage in their confrontation with the insurance companies (Adout 2002).

17. Patients' Rights Law, 1996, Article 3(B). As defined in this law, a medical emergency consists of "circumstances in which a person's life is in immediate danger, or when there is immediate danger that a person will incur severe and irreversible disability if he is not given urgent medical treatment." According to statistics from Ichilov hospital in Tel Aviv, bad debts in 2001 totaled 1.1 million NIS, and the accumulated debt over the years totals almost 5 million NIS.

18. For old Labor party members such as Namir, the migrant workers' phenomenon was especially unsettling. The return of the Jewish people to "productive" manual work was a main theme of socialist Zionism. "Importing" foreign workers to fill manual jobs was seen as a failure (a view that ignored the fact that since 1967 most manual, partially skilled work was done by Palestinians from the Occupied Territories).

19. This estimation does not include those children who received permanent residence through the government decision of 2007.

20. By January 2002, 1,016 families were receiving preventive care at the Tel Aviv mother-and-child clinics.

21. See Introduction.

22. Of the HIV/AIDS migrant patients currently registered at the Open Clinic and at the Israel AIDS Task Force, approximately 70% are women. Almost half the women were diagnosed as carriers on arriving in hospital to give birth or during monitoring of their pregnancy at the mother-and-child clinics.

23. In order to increase the therapeutic effect, AIDS therapy consists of a combination of different reverse-transcriptase inhibitors.

24. In accordance with the Ministry of Health regulations, drug companies running trials on new drugs must continue to supply the drug to the participants in the research for three years after its conclusion, unless it has not been proved effective. The participants in the said trials indeed continued to receive the drugs, but these periods of extension have expired.

5. The Occupation as the Ultimate Violation of the Right to Health

1. Even though Israel had begun to prepare plans for the administration of the West Bank and the Gaza Strip for any "contingency" several years before the war (Gordon 2008).

2. As mentioned in chapter 4, as CEO of the Clalit Sick Fund in the early 2000s, Peterburg was responsible for the "enterprization" of Clalit; i.e., the adoption of an institutional culture imported from the business sector. His success in the neoliberalization of the biggest sick fund opened for him the gates of the business world, and after leaving Clalit he was appointed CEO of Celcom, Israel's biggest cellular phone company. Figures such as Peterburg embody the relationship between the institutional skeleton of the occupation and the neoliberalization process.

3. This was so especially since the early 1990s.

4. On September 13, 1993, representatives of the State of Israel and the Palestine Liberation Organization (PLO) signed the Declaration of Principles on Interim Self-Government

Arrangements, also known as the Declaration of Principles (DOP) or Oslo Accords (they were finalized in Oslo, Norway, in August 1990). The Accords set out mutually agreed-upon general principles regarding a five-year interim period of Palestinian self-rule.

5. The Israeli-Palestinian Interim Agreement on the West Bank and the Gaza Strip was signed in Washington, DC, in 1995, and dealt with the capacities and powers of the Palestinian Authority's institutions, the IDF redeployment, and security issues.

6. Per capita government expenditure was much lower than expenditure in Egypt ($48), Syria ($90), and Jordan ($123) (Pfeiffer 2001).

7. In September 2000, following a visit of Ariel Sharon, the Likud party's chairperson at the time, to the Temple Mount/site of the Alaqsa mosque, an uprising began of the Palestinian population in the OPT. The Israeli violent repression fueled the Palestinian reaction, and the conflict rapidly escalated, putting an end to the Oslo process.

8. Saint Luke's hospital in Nablus, for example, reported a 49% decline in general practitioners' patients, a 73% decline in specialty services, and a 53% decline in surgery—at a time when needs had grown and there were an insufficient number of hospital beds (WHO 2002). Hospitals in East Jerusalem suffered especially badly from these restrictions because a significant proportion of their staff are residents of the West Bank (Ziv 2002).

9. The term "Green Line" is used to refer to the pre–Six Days War border between Israel and the Arab countries, defined in the 1949 Armistice. This border does not include the Golan Heights, the West Bank, and the Gaza Strip, occupied by Israel following the war.

10. According to the Oslo agreements, the DCOs would coordinate Israeli and Palestinian security arrangements.

11. For a report on damage inflicted on ambulances and medical services, see Ziv 2002.

12. The Islamic Jihad is a fundamentalist Islamic group founded in the Gaza Strip in the late 1970s by Fathi Shaqaqi as a branch of the Egyptian Islamic Jihad and is the most radical Palestinian organization.

13. Fatah is the major faction of the Palestinian Liberation Organization and one of the major Palestinian parties. It was the main political party until the 2005 elections and was the main Palestinian force involved in the Oslo process and the constitution of the Palestinian authority.

14. As of October 2007, the stock for 66 of 416 drugs on the essential drugs list was down to only 1 to 3 months' supply (OCHA 2007).

15. The Rafah border was closed in June 2006 and sporadically opened for an average of six days per month. On June 9, 2007, the border crossing was completely closed.

16. During January–May 2007, the monthly average number of requests for permits to cross Erez checkpoint for inpatient and outpatient health care services in hospitals in the West Bank, East Jerusalem, and Israel was 625, and the average number of people granted permits was 542. In June 2007, the number of requests for permits decreased to 413 because of the complete closure of Gaza Strip during the period of the Hamas takeover of the Gaza Strip. 369 of the requests were denied. The number of requests went up again during the period July–September 2007, and the average number of requests for permits reached 857; of these, 718 requests were granted permits (OCHA 2007).

Conclusion

1. This would mean the real fulfillment of the normalization promise embodied in Zionism and liberation from the ethnocultural definition imposed on the Jews by nineteenth-century European ethnonationalism

Bibliography

Abu Gosh, H., et al. 2007. Diabetes control in three villages in Palestine. *Journal of Ambulatory Care Management* 30:74–78.

Abu Saad, I., et al. 1999. *A Way Ahead: Development Plan for the Bedouin Towns in the Negev.* Beer Sheva: Center for the Study of the Bedouin Society.

Adout, R. 2002. *Violent Apathy: The Health Status of Migrant Workers—'Foreign Workers'—in Israel.* Tel Aviv: Physicians for Human Rights.

Agger, B. 1985. The Dialectic of Deindustrialization: An Essay on Advanced Capitalism. In *Critical Theory and Public Life,* ed. J. Forester. Cambridge, MA: MIT Press.

Alami, O. 2003. *No Man's Land—Health in the Unrecognized Villages of the Negev.* Tel Aviv: Physicians for Human Rights (PHR).

——. 2006. *Water Discipline.* Tel Aviv: PHR.

Alexander, M. 2007. Municipal Policies in Comparative Perspective: Understanding Tel Aviv's Policy Response to the Labor Migrant Phenomenon. In *Transational Migration to Israel in Global Comparative Context,* ed. S. Willen. Plymouth: Lexington Books.

Al-Haq. 1993. *An Ailing System: Israeli Military Government Health Insurance in the OPT.* Ramallah: Al-Haq.

Al-Krenawi, A., et al. 2004. *Psycho-social Challenges of Indigenous Societies.* Beer Sheba: Ben Gurion University (Hebrew).

Bank of Israel. 2005. *Annual Report.* Jerusalem: Bank of Israel.

Bantram, D. V. 1998. "Foreign workers in Israel: History and theory." *International Migration Review* 32:303–325.

Barnea, T., and R. Husseini. 2002. *Separate and Cooperate, Cooperate and Separate: The Disengagement of the Palestinian Health Care System from Israel and Its Emergence as an Independent System.* Victoria: Praeger Books.

Barghouti, M., and I. Daibes. 1993. *Infrastructure and Health Services in the West Bank: Guidelines for Health Care Planning.* Ramallah: Health Development Information Project.

Berg A., B. Rosen, and B. Morgenstern. 2002. *Differences between Lower and Middle Income People after the Legislation of the National Health Insurance Law.* Jerusalem: Brookdale-JDC (Hebrew).

Bin Nun, G. 1999. Cost and sources of the basket of services of the NHI law. *Social Security* 54:35–53 (Hebrew).

Bin Nun, G., and D. Chinitz. 1993. The Roles of Government and the Market in the Israeli Health-Care System in the 1980s. In *The Changing Role of Government and the Market in Health Care Systems,* ed. D. Chinitz and M. Cohen. Jerusalem: JDC-Brookdale and Ministry of Health.

Bin Nun G., and S. Greenblat. 1999. *Distribution of Insurees Among Israeli Health Insurance Funds (Sick Funds) 1950–1998.* Jerusalem: Ministry of Health (Hebrew).

Borkan, J., et al. 2000. Universal health care? The views of Negev Bedouin Arabs on health services. *Health Policy and Planning* 15:207–217.

Central Bureau of Statistics (CBS). 1993. *Use of Health Services Survey.* Jerusalem: CBS (Hebrew).

——. 1995. *Census of Population and Housing.* Jerusalem: CBS (Hebrew).

——. 1998. *Health and Health Resources in Israel.* Jerusalem: CBS (Hebrew).

——. 1998b. *Jubilee Publications: Economic Industries, Manufacturing, Commerce and Services.* Jerusalem: CBS (Hebrew).

——. 1999. *Statistical Abstract of Israel.* Jerusalem: CBS.

——. 2000. *Statistical Yearbook.* Jerusalem: CBS.

——. 2001. *Statistical Yearbook.* Jerusalem: CBS.

——. 2003. *Statistical Yearbook.* Jerusalem: CBS.

——. 2005. *Statistical Yearbook.* Jerusalem: CBS.

——. 2006. *National Health Survey.* Jerusalem: CBS.

——. 2007. *Statistical Yearbook.* Jerusalem: CBS.

Chernichovsky, D. 1991. *Economic Dimensions of the Crisis in the Israeli Health-care System.* Jerusalem: JDC-Brookdale (Hebrew).

Chinitz, D. 1995. Israel's health policy breakthrough: The politics of reform and the reform of politics. *Journal of Health Policy, Politics and Law* 20:904–932.

Chinitz, D., and B. Rosen. 1991. *Patterns of Hospital Competition in Israel in Early 1990.* Jerusalem: JDC-Brookdale (Hebrew).

Chernichowski D., et al. 2003. *Capitation System and Allocation of Resources for Health Care Services in Israel.* Jerusalem: Centre for the Study of Public Policies (Hebrew).

Cwikel, J., and N. Barak. 2003. *Health and Welfare of Bedouin Women in the Negev.* Beer Sheva: Centre for the Study of Bedouin Society (Hebrew).

Daibes, I., and M. Barghouti. 1996. *Infrastructure and Health Service in the Gaza Strip: The Gaza Strip Primary Health Care Survey.* Ramallah: The Health Development Information Project.

Davidi, E. 2000. Globalization and economy in the Middle East. *Palestine-Israel Journal* 7:33–38.

Dohan, L. 2001. Principal Causes of Death among Non-Jewish Babies in 1999. In *Mobile Service for Mothers and Children in the Bedouin Sector in the Southern Region.* Beer Sheva: Regional Health Office—Southern Region (Hebrew).

Esping-Andersen, G. 1990. *The Three Worlds of Welfare Capitalism.* Princeton, NJ: Princeton University Press.

Filc, D. 2004. Israel Model 2000: Neo-Liberal Post-Fordism. In *The Power of Property: Israeli Society in the Global Age,* ed. D. Filc and U. Ram. Jerusalem: Van Leer Institute for Advanced Study and Hakibbutz Hameuchad (Hebrew).

———. 2004b. Foreword in *The Bureaucracy of Occupation: The District Civil Liaison Offices.* Tel Aviv: MachsomWatch and PHR.

Filc, D., and N. Davidovitch. 2005. Health care as a national right? The development of health care services for migrant workers in Israel. *Social Theory and Health* 3:1–15.

Freeman, G. 1992. The Consequence of Immigration Policies for Immigrant Status: A British and French Comparison. In *Ethnic and Racial Minorities in Advanced Industrial Democracies,* ed. A. Messina et al. New York: Greenwood Press.

Frevert U. 1985. Professional medicine and the working classes in imperial Germany. *Journal of Contemporary History* 20:637–658.

Gal, J. 1994. Privatization of services in the welfare state: The Israeli case. *Society and Welfare* 15:7–24 (Hebrew).

Gazit, M. 2000. The genesis of the US–Israeli military-strategic relationship and the Dimona issue. *Journal of Contemporary History* 35:413–422.

Giacaman, R., et al. 2004. Imprints on the consciousness: The impact on Palestinian civilians of the Israeli Army invasion of West Bank towns. *European Journal of Public Health* 14:286–290.

Gordon, N. 2008 *Israel's Occupation.* Berkeley: University of California Press.

Gordon, N., and D. Filc. 2005. Hamas and the destruction of risk society. *Constellations* 12:544–562.

Gordon N., R. Mazali, and N. Ofer. 1993. *The Occupied Health Care System.* Tel Aviv: Physicians for Human Rights.

Gottlieb, N. 2006. Accessibility and utilization of antenatal care among the Arab Bedouin of the unrecognized villages of the Negev desert. Master's thesis, Ben Gurion University.

Greenberg, D. 1983. Health care in Israel. *New England Journal of Medicine* 309: 681–684.

Gross R., S. Barmeli-Greenberg, and B. Rosen. 2007. Co-payments: The implications for service accessibility and equity. *Law and Business* 6:197–225 (Hebrew).

Halevy, H. 1980. *The Bumpy Road to National Health Insurance: The Case of Israel.* Jerusalem: Brookdale-JDC.

Hamdan, M., and M. Defever. 2003. Human resources for health in Palestine, a policy analysis. *Health Policy* 64:243–259.

Hindess, B. 1993. Citizenship in the Modern State. In Citizenship and Social Theory, ed. B. Turner. London: Sage.

Hobbes, T. 1958. *Leviathan.* Oxford: Clarendon.

Izreeli, D., and N. Yalin. 1999. *Health-care Costs by Ethnicity.* Tel Aviv: Kupat Holim Clalit (Hebrew).

Kawachi, I., and B. Kennedy. 2002. *The Health of Nations: Why Inequality Is Harmful to Your Health.* New York: New Press.

Kemp, A., and R. Rajman, 2004. *Foreign Workers in Israel.* Tel Aviv: Information on Equality, Adva Center.

———. 2007. Labor Migration, Managing the Ethno-National Conflict, and Client Politics in Israel. In *Transnational Migration to Israel in Global Comparative Context,* ed. S. Willen. Lanham, MD: Lexington Books.

Kimhi, I. 2006. The Separation Wall's Influence Over the Palestinian Residents in Jerusalem and the Metropolitan Area. In *Security Fence in Jerusalem,* ed. I. Kimhi. Jerusalem: Jerusalem Centre for the Study of Israel.

Kimhi, I., and M. Hoshen. 2006. The Separation Wall's Influence Over the Inhabitants of the Arab Villages Near Jerusalem. In *Security Fence in Jerusalem,* ed. I. Kimhi. Jerusalem: Jerusalem Centre for the Study of Israel.

Kimmerling, B. 2004. *Immigrants, Settlers, Natives: State and Society in Israel.* Tel Aviv: Am Oved (Hebrew).

Kordysh, E., et al. 2005. Respiratory morbidity in hospitalized Bedouins residing near an industrial park. *Archives of Environmental and Occupational Health* 60:147–155.

Kuminsky, G. 2008. Health care reform in the USA. Paper presented in the workshop, Assessing Health Care Reforms: Europe, USA and Israel, Ben Gurion University.

Lain, Y. 2004. *The Regime of Forbidden Roads in the West Bank.* Jerusalem: B'tselem (Hebrew).

Lewando-Hundt, G., et al. 2001. Knowledge, action, and resistance: The selective use of pre-natal screening among Bedouin women of the Negev, Israel. *Social Science and Medicine* 5:561–569.

Light, D. 1997. From managed competition to managed cooperation: Theory and lessons from the British experience. *The Milbank Quarterly* 75:3.

Little, D. 1993. The making of a special relationship: The United States and Israel, 1957–68. *International Journal of Middle East Studies* 25:563–585.

Mataria, A., R. Giacaman, R. Khalib, and JP Moatti. 2006. Impoverishment and patients' "willingness" and "ability" to pay for improving the quality of health care in Palestine: an assessment using the contingent valuation method. *Health Policy* 75:312–318.

Ministry of Finance. 2005. Budget 2005. www.mof.gov.il.

Ministry of Health. 1998. *Highlights of the Israeli Health-care System.* Jerusalem: Ministry of Health (Hebrew).

Ministry of Industry and Commerce. 2004. Newsletter 41. Jerusalem: Ministry of Industry and Commerce (Hebrew).

Ministry of Interior. 2005. *The Ministry of Interior Readiness to Deal with the Bedouins in the Southern Region.* Beer Sheva: Ministry of Interior (Hebrew).

Morad, A., et al. 2006. The influence of Israel health insurance law on the Negev Bedouin population, a survey study. *Scientific World Journal* 6:81–95.

Moss, N. 2002. Gender equity and socioeconomic inequality: A framework for the patterning of women's health. *Social Science and Medicine* 54:649–661.

National Health Insurance Law. 1994. http://web1.nevo.co.il/Law_word/law01/036_001.doc (Hebrew).

Office for the Coordination of Humanitarian Affairs. 2007. *Gaza Humanitarian Situation Report. Jerusalem: OCHA.*

Oxfam. 2007. *Breaking the Impasse: Ending the Humanitarian Stranglehold on Palestine.* http://www.oxfam.org.uk/resources/policy/conflict_disasters/downloads/bn_palestine.pdf.

Palti, H. 1996. The National Health Insurance law: Its reflections on the mother and child health preventive services. *Social Services* 47:89–95 (Hebrew).

Pappe, I. 2004. *A History of Modern Palestine: One Land, Two Peoples.* Cambridge: Cambridge University Press.

Peled, Y. 1992. Strangers in the Utopia: The Citizen Status of Palestinians in Israel. *Theory and Critique* 3:21–33 (Hebrew).

Pessate-Schubert, A. 2003. Changing from the margins: Bedouin women and higher education in Israel. *Women's Studies International Forum* 4:285–298.

Peterburg, Y. 2001. A Clinic Without Frontiers. In *Time for Medicine,* ed. Israel Medical Association. Tel Aviv: IMA (Hebrew).

Peterburg, Y., and Y. Sever. 2002. Development and Provision by Israel of Health Care Services for the Palestinians in the West Bank and the Gaza Strip between 1967 and 1994. In *Separate and Cooperate, Cooperate and Separate: The Disengagement of the Palestine Health Care System from Israel and Its Emergence as an Independent System,* ed. T. Barnea and R. Husseini. Westport: Praeger Publishers.

Pfeiffer, M. 2001. *Vulnerability and the International Health Response in the West Bank and Gaza Strip: An Analysis of Health and the Health Sector.* Jerusalem: WHO. Palestinian Ministry of Health. 2000. *Annual Report.* Ramallah: PMH.

———. 2003. *Annual Report.* Ramallah: PMH.

Porat, C. 1993. The contribution of Ben Gurion's geographic-settlement conception on the settlement of the Negev and its development during the first years of the state. *Studies on Israel's Reconstruction* 3:114–143 (Hebrew).

Qouta, O., et al. 2003. Prevalence and determinants of PTSD among Palestinian children exposed to military violence. *European Child and Adolescent Psychiatry* 12:265–272.

Ram, U. 2007. *The Globalization of Israel, McWorld in Tel Aviv, Jihad in Jerusalem.* London: Routledge.

Reiss, N. 1988. *Health Services to the Arab Population in Israel.* Tel Aviv: International Center for Peace in the Middle East.

Rigby, A. 1991. Coping with the "epidemic of violence": The struggle over health care in the Intifada. *Journal of Palestine Studies* 20:86–98.

Rosen, B., et al. 1995. *Consumer Behavior in the Sick Fund Market.* Jerusalem: JDC-Brookdale (Hebrew).

Rosenhek, Z. 2000. Migration regimes, Intra-state conflicts, and the politics of exclusion and inclusion: Migrant workers in the Israeli welfare wtate. *Social Problems* 47:49–67.

——. 2003. The political dynamics of a segmented labour market: Palestinian citizens, Palestinians from the Occupied Territories, and migrant workers in Israel. *Acta Sociologica* 46:151–169.

——. 2007. Conclusion: Challenging Exclusionary Migration Regimes: Labor Migration in Israel in Comparative Perspective. In *Transational Migration to Israel in Global Comparative Context,* ed. S. Willen. Plymouth: Lexington Books.

Rytter J., et al. 2006. Effects of armed conflict on access to emergency health care in Palestinian West Bank: Systematic collection of data in emergency departments. *British Medical Journal* 332:1122–1124.

Segev, T. 1991. *The Seventh Million: The Israelis and the Holocaust.* New York: Henry Holt and Company.

——. 2001. *One Palestine, Complete: Jews and Arabs under the British Mandate.* New York: Metropolitan Books.

——. 2002. *Elvis in Jerusalem: Post-Zionism and the Americanization of Israel.* New York: Metropolitan Books.

Semyonov, M., and N. Lewin-Epstein. 1992. Local labor markets, ethnic segregation, and income inequality. *Social Forces* 70 (4):1101–1119.

——. 1994. Sheltered labor markets, public sector employment and socio-economic returns to education of Arabs in Israel. *American Journal of Sociology* 100:622–651.

Sered, S. 2000. *What Makes Women Sick? Maternity, Modesty, and Militarism in Israeli Society.* Hanover, NH: University Press of New England.

Shafir, G., and Y. Peled. 2002. *Being Israeli: The Dynamics of Multiple Citizenships.* Cambridge: Cambridge University Press.

Shalev, H., et al. 2006. Murine typhus is a common cause of febrile illness in Bedouin children in Israel. *Scandinavian Journal of Infectious Diseases* 38:451–455.

Shalom, N., and M. Harison. 1996. Strategical changes in public hospitals as a consequence of health-care system reform. *Social Security* 47:152–167 (Hebrew).

Shirom, A. 1993. Toward a Diagnostic Model of Macro-systems in the Public Sector: The Case of Israel's Health-Care System. In *The Changing Role of Government and the Market in Health Care Systems,* ed. D. Chinitz and M. Cohen. Jerusalem: JDC-Brookdale and MOH.

Shirom, A., and Z. Amit. 1996. Private-public mix in state-owned general hospitals: An assessment of the present status and future developments. *Social Security* 47:48–70 (Hebrew).

Shlaim, A. 2001. *The Iron Wall: Israel and the Arab World.* London: W.W. Norton.

Shmueli, A. 2000. Inequality in medical care in Israel: Arabs and Jews in the Jerusalem district of the Jerusalem sick fund. *European Journal of Public Health* 10 (1): 18–24.

Shoam-Vardi, I. 2004. *Infant Mortality Among the Bedouin Population of the Negev Presentation on the Project for Reduction of IMR among the Negev Bedouin Population.* Beer Sheva: Ben-Gurion University of the Negev (Hebrew).

Shuval, J. 1992. *Social Dimensions of Health: The Israeli Experience.* Westport: Prager.

Swirski, B., et al. 1998. *Equality Monitor: Health.* Tel Aviv: Adva Center (Hebrew).

Swirski, S. 2005. *The Price of Occupation.* Tel Aviv: Adva Center.

——. 2006. *Invisible Citizens.* Tel Aviv: Adva Center.

Swissa, S. 2003. *Harm to Medical Personnel: The Delay, Abuse and Humiliation of Medical Personnel by Israeli Security Forces.* Tel Aviv: Betzelem and Physicians for Human Rights.

Szymborska, W. 2000. Orlando: Harvest Press.

Tulchinsky, T., and G. Ginsberg. 1996. *A District Health Profile of Beer Sheva Sub-district (the Negev).* Jerusalem: MOH.

Turner, B. 1993. *Citizenship and Social Theory.* London: Sage.

United Nations. 1989. Convention on the Rights of the Child, General Assembly resolution 44/25.

United Nations Relief and Work Agency for Palestine Refugees in the Middle East. 2005. *UNRWA in 2005.* Gaza: UNRWA.

UNRWA. 2007. *Annual Report of the Department of Health.* Gaza: UNRWA.

Wilkinson, R. 1996. *Unhealthy Societies: The Afflictions of Inequality.* London: Routledge.

Willen, S. 2003. Perspectives on labour migration in Israel. *Revue Européenne des Migrations Internationales* 19:243–262.

———. 2007. Introduction. In *Transational Migration to Israel in Global Comparative Context,* ed. S. Willen. Plymouth: Lexington Books.

Weingarten, M., and H. Ziv. 2003. *Report on a Visit to the Villages of Salem, Deir al Hatab and Azmut.* Tel Aviv: PHR.

World Bank. 2003. *World Bank Report on Intifadah.* World Bank Report Number 26313.

———. 2004. *Deep Palestinian Poverty in the Midst of Economic Crisis.* West Bank and Gaza, World Bank Report Number 30751.

———. 2006. *The Impeding Palestinian Fiscal Crisis, Potential Remedies.* World Bank Report Number 43063.

World Health Organization. 1978. *Declaration of Alma Ata.* Geneva: WHO.

———. 2004. *World Health Report.* Geneva: WHO.

Yahav-KHC. 1998. *TTT: Train The Trainer.* Tel Aviv: KHC (Hebrew).

Yiftahel, O. 2000. *Lands, Planning and Inequality: The Distribution of Space between Jews and Arabs in Israel.* Tel Aviv: Adva Center.

Ziv, H. 2002. *Medicine Under Attack Critical Damage Inflicted on Medical Services in the Occupied Territories: An Interim Report.* Tel Aviv: PHR.

———. 2003. *The Bureaucracy of Occupation: The District Civil Liaison Offices.* Tel Aviv: MachsomWatch and PHR.

Ziv, H., et al. 2003. Conflict and public health: Report from Physicians for Human Rights–Israel. *The Lancet* 361:1221.

INDEX

The names of individual patients used in this text (e.g. Alejandro, Zahra) will be found under the entry "case study subjects."